NEW DIRECTIONS FOR HIGHER EDUCATION

Martin Kramer
EDITOR-IN-CHIEF

# Preparing Competent College Graduates: Setting New and Higher Expectations for Student Learning

Elizabeth A. Jones
*The Pennsylvania State University*

EDITOR

Number 96, Winter 1996

JOSSEY-BASS PUBLISHERS
San Francisco

PREPARING COMPETENT COLLEGE GRADUATES: SETTING NEW AND HIGHER
EXPECTATIONS FOR STUDENT LEARNING
*Elizabeth A. Jones* (ed.)
New Directions for Higher Education, no. 96
Volume XXIV, Number 4
*Martin Kramer*, Editor-in-Chief

ISSN 0271-0560      ISBN 0-7879-9823-0   *June 9, 1997*

NEW DIRECTIONS FOR HIGHER EDUCATION is part of The Jossey-Bass
Higher and Adult Education Series and is published quarterly by Jossey-
Bass Inc., Publishers, 350 Sansome Street, San Francisco, California
94104-1342. Periodicals postage paid at San Francisco, California, and at
additional mailing offices. POSTMASTER: Send address changes to New
Directions for Higher Education, Jossey-Bass Inc., Publishers, 350 Sansome Street, San Francisco, California 94104-1342.

SUBSCRIPTIONS cost $52.00 for individuals and $79.00 for institutions,
agencies, and libraries.

EDITORIAL CORRESPONDENCE should be sent to the Editor-in-Chief, Martin
Kramer, 2807 Shasta Road, Berkeley, California 94708-2011.

Cover photograph and random dot by Richard Blair/Color & Light © 1990.

Jossey-Bass Web address: http://www.josseybass.com

TCF   Manufactured in the United States of America on Lyons Falls
Pathfinder Tradebook. This paper is acid-free and 100 percent
totally chlorine-free.

# CONTENTS

# EDITOR'S NOTES

Today there is widespread concern and discontent with the quality of educational programs and levels of student achievement. In order to evaluate educational quality, we must examine curricular and pedagogical issues that are tied to our expectations, teaching practices, learning outcomes, and interactions among stakeholders in the academic community. To assess quality, we must first set clear, explicit goals for student learning outcomes and share these aims with our students, colleagues, and other stakeholder groups on a regular basis. While many program faculty and general education committees find defining goals to be a difficult part of the assessment process, they also find it to be the most productive part (Wolff, 1990). [Structured, ongoing dialogues among faculty about educational goals, objectives, and criteria create cultures with an emphasis on learning outcomes. Such cultures bring to the forefront important assumptions of individual faculty that are often never discussed with colleagues. Decisions about learning outcomes and some degree of consensus among faculty (for example, within a particular major) can lead to greater clarity, coherence, and focus within academic programs and general education.]

The articulation of higher expectations for student learning is not sufficient alone to raise student achievement. However, clear statements about the intended outcomes should help shape the teaching and evaluation practices in the classroom while actual assessments provide data about the attainment of these outcomes.

Recently, the National Center for Education Statistics (NCES) commissioned three national studies through the National Center on Postsecondary Teaching, Learning, and Assessment (Jones and others, 1994; Jones, Dougherty, and Fantaske, 1997). As the principal investigator, I led a team of researchers in identifying the specific skills and levels of learning that college graduates should master to be effective in the workplace and in society. NCES asked investigators to focus specifically on critical reading, writing, speaking, listening, problem solving, and critical thinking. Prior to our study, NCES convened several working groups to identify learning expectations and assessment issues regarding these skills. Individual authors were commissioned to write position papers representing the most recent debates and ideas in their fields. We used these documents and conducted extensive literature reviews to develop five goals inventories (Jones, 1994, 1996). These instruments outline both basic and advanced skills that college graduates should achieve. Teamwork, collaboration, and an understanding and openness toward diversity are important abilities embedded within these inventories, because they are an integral part of effective communications and critical thinking. In addition, many of these skills are interrelated. The ability to make reasoned judgments is an integral part of the reading, writing, speaking, and listening processes.

Collectively, these skills represent iterative, nonlinear processes that allow for reflection, exploration, and revision before decisions are made or before final products are delivered.

Advisory boards of employers, faculty, and policymakers reviewed and critiqued draft surveys. In addition, focus groups met and evaluated these instruments. Then we sent these inventories to more than 600 individuals (employers who hire college graduates, faculty from different disciplines, and policymakers, including members of accrediting organizations, boards of trustees, and state-level higher education coordinating boards). After we collected and analyzed the data, we identified specific areas of agreement and disagreement among the stakeholder groups (Jones, 1994, 1996). The results from this research were inventory lists of key skills in communications, critical thinking, and problem solving that faculty, employers, and policymakers agree college graduates should possess. These inventories help faculty and academic administrators think more specifically about the learning experiences necessary to engender such abilities in their students. They can help employers to be more specific about their expectations regarding the skills they are looking for as they recruit and hire college graduates.

This study does not provide a single definition of important skills and abilities; rather, it was intended to stimulate discussions about these extensive lists of goals so that faculty may adapt, modify, and decide which expectations are most appropriate for their own undergraduates. A strength of our modern colleges and universities is that they provide a universe of knowledge and curricula that mirror our complex and diverse society. Such curricular complexity is necessary given the diversity of students with different goals, interests, aspirations, and expectations. Assessments must reflect and describe the diversity of the curriculum if they are to enhance our students' abilities.

In this volume, the authors address specific outcomes we should expect from our college graduates. They evaluate the results of our national study and discuss the implications for faculty and administrators responsible for the improvement of educational programs.

There are several underlying assumptions that cut across these chapters. The development of communication, critical thinking, and problem solving are the responsibility of faculty who teach general education and courses for the majors. There are better ways to embed these clearer and higher expectations for student learning in courses *across* the curriculum. These expectations should be communicated on a regular basis. They include not only basic skills but skills at more advanced levels. Although some faculty in our national study asserted that basic skills have no place in the undergraduate curriculum, many employers told us that their new employees (with college degrees) often had weak communication skills and lacked other fundamental skills. Therefore, the instruction and assessment of both basic and advanced levels of learning are crucial in higher education. The acquisition of knowledge is important as a foundation, but the real issue is whether an undergraduate can use that knowledge to make reasoned judgments and can apply it to a range of contexts and issues. These skills are equally important to develop for both the workplace and society. Critical thinking is vital, because college graduates must make difficult judgments about many political debates and consider different viewpoints about many public issues. The refinement of these skills does not end with attainment of a college degree. College graduates have multiple roles in the workplace and in society, where they have opportunities to use these skills and to receive further training, often through structured workforce programs, continuing education or professional development seminars, or involvement in different community activities. Collectively, these chapters represent work and initiatives aimed at setting more explicit expectations for student learning that are informed by society's expectations.

In Chapter One, I review the major external initiatives under way that have an impact on the development of expectations for student learning. Many reports from scholars, the professions, and other organizations analyze weaknesses within the undergraduate curriculum and make recommendations for improvement. Formal research studies document the importance of communication and critical thinking skills for employment and career mobility. Similar skills are equally important for undergraduates to effectively participate in our democratic society. The policies of accrediting organizations and state-level higher education coordinating boards have also stimulated reforms in undergraduate education. Despite these external influences, many faculty and administrators are becoming more active in defining, implementing, and evaluating their own plans to determine the quality of their educational programs and student learning at their own institutions.

In Chapter Two, Rebecca Rubin and Sherwyn Morreale describe how college students can achieve communication competence. Both authors have served as chair of the Speech Communication Association's committee on assessment and testing. They suggest ways that undergraduates can make decisions about what is appropriate and effective in different communication situations. They review specific basic and advanced skills that should be developed by undergraduates. These perspectives are informed by the Speech Communication Association and national studies. They recommend numerous approaches for effectively teaching these skills and offer guidelines for assessing oral communication.

The ability to write clearly and effectively is another challenge for undergraduates. In Chapter Three, Benjamin Click reviews essential writing skills that college graduates need to master to communicate with diverse audiences. He reviews three different theoretical approaches for writing instruction, and summarizes employers', policymakers', and faculty's expectations. Although there is much agreement in our national study (Jones, 1994), many faculty view writing as an iterative process (one that involves drafting and revising), while most employers are primarily concerned with the final product and its quality.

College-level reading requires undergraduates to understand texts and to effectively interpret, analyze, and judge the ideas contained in various documents.

In Chapter Four, JoAnn Carter-Wells analyzes diverse theoretical frameworks for reading outcomes and current workplace issues. She also summarizes the critical reading portion of our national research study (Jones, 1996) and discusses implications for policy, curriculum design, teaching, learning, and assessment.

When college students enter the workplace, they are faced with many choices and complex information as they strive to solve unfamiliar problems. In Chapter Five, Christopher Dougherty and Patti Fantaske examine diverse frameworks that articulate the problem-solving process and are based upon cognitive psychology studies. They review the major methods associated with effective resolution of problems and explore the ways these skills are articulated in the professions, as well as in selected disciplines. They also highlight effective strategies for teaching problem solving.

While college graduates may possess strong problem-solving or critical thinking skills, they must be inclined to follow through with behaviors corresponding to these skills. The development of attitudes, preferences, and intentions is crucial as diversity in the workforce and in society increases. Peter A. Facione, Noreen C. Facione, and Carol Ann F. Giancarlo assert in Chapter Six that undergraduates as learners and workers must be willing and motivated to make informed, skilled, and fair-minded judgments as they solve problems or make decisions. They illustrate key habits of mind that demonstrate the consistent internal motivation to use one's critical thinking abilities in deciding what to believe or do in specific situations. The authors have developed a dispositions inventory, and they summarize recent research studies involving the use of their instrument. They recommend five principles that may lead to a stronger nurturing of the disposition toward critical thinking.

In addition to these extremely important skills, learning to use technology can provide undergraduates with opportunities to develop their reflection, thinking, and collaborative skills. In Chapter Seven, Ann Deden and Vicki K. Carter outline the major challenges associated with the effective use of new technologies. They offer a rich array of innovative technology initiatives and pilot projects under way at certain colleges and universities. Many of these innovations are fairly recent, so few longitudinal evaluations exist to provide hard data on improved student performance. However, these models may help improve instructional effectiveness and, ultimately, student learning.

Key skills and abilities are also taught and developed further in the workplace. In Chapter Eight, Thomas T. Wojcik discusses a model for innovation that has been implemented at the Hoechst Celanese Corporation. That company's Office of Innovation has created a series of initiatives aimed at helping employees discover and evaluate new ideas and explore alternatives. Employees learn how to transform their ideas into business concept proposals and how to make key judgments as they compose their business plans. These examples illustrate how teamwork and relationship building, rather than individual efforts, are fostered in the workplace. In addition, several initiatives are aimed at strengthening customer relationships.

The development of clear expectations and learning outcomes is not sufficient to enhance undergraduate learning. Instructional practices need to be reviewed, and good practices should be incorporated into the college classroom. In the last chapter, Carole Barrowman asserts that when faculty make public their expectations for student learning, and they use those expectations to navigate their teaching, students can be better prepared for life. She offers examples from the Alverno College curriculum that illustrate innovative practices connecting faculty expectations for student learning with teaching and assessment practices. Barrowman particularly focuses on the process for defining expectations and how these expectations reshape teaching and learning to bring coherence to the undergraduate curriculum.

Much of the research reported in this volume (particularly in Chapters One through Six) has been generously supported by a grant from the National Center for Education Statistics (NCES) in the Office of Educational Research and Improvement, through the U.S. Department of Education. This research was conducted through the National Center on Postsecondary Teaching, Learning, and Assessment at The Pennsylvania State University. Dr. Salvatore Corrallo was the program officer in the NCES who provided great enthusiasm and good advice about future directions. This work would not have been possible without the guidance and consultations with our advisory boards and focus groups in critical thinking, problem solving, reading, writing, and speech communications. These faculty, employers, and policymakers volunteered their time to critique our work during the course of this project. I would also like to thank the reviewers for their comments and suggestions about this volume. While we are grateful to these sponsors and individuals, the analyses and interpretations presented here remain solely those of the authors.

Elizabeth A. Jones<br>
Editor

## References

Jones, E. A. *Critical Thinking, Writing, Speaking, and Listening Goals Inventories.* University Park: National Center on Postsecondary Teaching, Learning, and Assessment, The Pennsylvania State University, 1994.

Jones, E. A. *Problem-Solving and Critical Reading Goals Inventories.* University Park: National Center on Postsecondary Teaching, Learning, and Assessment, The Pennsylvania State University, 1996.

Jones, E. A., Dougherty, C., and Fantaske, P. *Essential Skills in Critical Reading and Problem Solving for College Graduates: Perspectives of Faculty, Employers, and Policymakers.* University Park: National Center on Postsecondary Teaching, Learning, and Assessment, The Pennsylvania State University, 1997.

Jones, E. A., Hoffman, S., Melander-Moore, L., Ratcliff, G., Tibbetts, S., and Click, B.A.L. *Essential Skills in Writing, Speech and Listening, and Critical Thinking for College Graduates: Perspectives of Faculty, Employers, and Policymakers.* University Park: National Center on

Postsecondary Teaching, Learning, and Assessment, The Pennsylvania State University, 1994.

Wolff, R. A. "Assessment and Accreditation: A Shotgun Marriage?" In *Assessment 1990: Accreditation and Renewal.* Washington, D.C.: The American Association of Higher Education Assessment Forum, 1990.

*ELIZABETH A. JONES was the principal investigator and project director of a series of national assessment projects. She is a research associate in the Center for the Study of Higher Education and assistant professor in the graduate higher education program at The Pennsylvania State University. She is also associate editor of the* Journal of General Education.

*Policies being articulated beyond the campus indicate what society expects undergraduates to learn.*

# National and State Policies Affecting Learning Expectations

*Elizabeth A. Jones*

Employers, policymakers, faculty, leaders in higher education, and the public all are concerned about the development of key cognitive abilities and communication skills of undergraduates. Employers are particularly troubled by weaknesses in new workers' skills. The inability of large numbers of employees to meet the reading, writing, or computational standards required by many segments of American business is an economic and competitive issue for U.S. companies challenged by foreign enterprises (Carnevale, Gainer, and Melzer, 1990). As a result, more corporations are trying to influence the U.S. educational system to improve the skills of future workers (Coates, Jarratt, and Mahaffie, 1990). In addition, state policymakers have developed new higher education accountability measures and expect information about the assessment of student performance and achievement of educational outcomes (Southern Regional Education Board, 1993). The public is more vocal in expressing its diminished trust in higher education as well as its belief that it is increasingly disconnected from important societal purposes (Southern Regional Education Board, 1993; Education Commission of the States, 1995). The public and other stakeholders in higher education want improvements in students' abilities to communicate effectively, think critically, and solve problems. Improvement of these skills is necessary to raise the quality of our workforce and to prepare educated citizens for our democratic society.

The need for college graduates to communicate effectively is very important in our society, where the daily operations and success of business organizations are contingent on making decisions, solving problems, and managing, documenting, and reporting large amounts of complex information. In nearly every study investigating the qualities employers most desire in their employees, "good communication skills, both verbal and written, rank high among the top priorities of those in business and industry" (Barabas, 1990, p. 9).

Recent research on job performance consistently indicates that attempts to itemize skills specific to certain occupations are inadequate; rather, it has underscored the role of communication and problem-solving skills as critical in rapidly changing job environments (College Placement Council, 1994; Carnevale, Gainer, and Meltzer, 1990). Although most employees enter new positions with adequate technical skills (for example, knowledge of accounting principles), it is the generic skills (especially communications and problem solving) that count toward successful job performance over time, and it is these skills that are most often absent (College Placement Council, 1994). In addition, college students view these skills as crucial and necessary to ensure their own career mobility (Education Commission of the States, 1995).

Similar skills and abilities are important to prepare college students for service and citizenship. Morse (1989) describes the civic skills needed for students to participate in public activities in our democracy. Political talk is important and includes a wide range of communications skills (Barber, 1984). Critical thinking is also necessary to learn civic responsibility (Glaser, 1985). Critical thinking includes a willingness to reflect on problems and issues, a knowledge of different methods of reasoning and critical inquiry, and the ability to apply those methods.

In this chapter, the major external organizational policies affecting the development of expectations for student learning and assessment efforts at colleges and universities are examined.

## National Reports

The academic community, employers, and policymakers continue to raise questions about the quality and effectiveness of undergraduate education. In the 1980s, a steady stream of reports called for education reforms and improvements. The authors of these documents expressed discontent with student learning and achievement. They asserted that changes at the borders of the curriculum were not sufficient to affect the quality of educational programs. Most of these authors called for major curriculum reforms of the entire undergraduate experience. For example, in *Integrity in the College Curriculum* (Association of American Colleges, 1985), the authors claimed that "evidence of decline and devaluation is everywhere. The business community complains of difficulty in recruiting literate college graduates" (p. 1). They stressed that the curriculum can be anything, and faculty were more confident about the length of a collegiate education than its content and purpose. The authors asserted that "the result is a loss of rigor in both secondary and in the collegiate course of study. That loss of definition and rigor has encouraged the false notion that there is such a thing as effortless learning, a notion that finds expression in curricular practices and student behavior" (p. 3). In a formal study to examine the claims in the *Integrity* report, Zemsky (1989) analyzed the coursework patterns of a large group of seniors from thirty colleges and universities. His findings supported the previous report's assertions. Zemsky found that there was a "notable absence of structure and coherence in the curriculum" (p. 7). His analyses indicated that there is a continued fragmentation of undergraduate education, which "ought to be greater than the sum of its parts" (p. 7).

Other groups expressed their concern with the quality of student learning and called for raising the levels of student abilities and skills (for example, Carnegie Foundation for the Advancement of Teaching, 1977; Boyer and Kaplan, 1977).

Whereas some authors concentrated on analyzing curriculum weaknesses, other authors proposed ways to overcome these challenges. Some authors were prescriptive and outlined their specific vision for the content and structure of an ideal curriculum (Cheney, 1989; Boyer and Levine, 1981; Bloom, 1987). Other proposals were less prescriptive, with scholars recommending that the general education curriculum should provide a strong foundation for undergraduates to develop certain key skills and abilities, including critical thinking, communications, and problem solving. Many of these authors stressed that formal, comprehensive evaluations and assessments were the key to determining the quality of an institution's curriculum and undergraduates' mastery of necessary skills and abilities. These authors argued that both students and faculty should be evaluated on a regular basis, including evaluations of the quality of teaching. These authors outlined perceptions of a mismatch between what society expects and what students can do that has stimulated a number of new initiatives designed to raise standards, change curricula, and restructure the ways institutions conduct business.

A number of art and science disciplines and their learned societies have also outlined the abilities that should be developed by students majoring in them, including critical inquiry, historical consciousness, scientific perspective, value assessment, aesthetic judgment, as well as disciplinary methods and knowledge (Association of American Colleges, 1991). The reports from these fields illustrate a shift away from the traditional notion that only content should be mastered, toward an emphasis on methods of interpretation and modes of judgment. All of the fields implicitly treated departmental majors as purposeful learning communities with a primary goal of helping undergraduates develop ways of thinking appropriate to that community (Schneider, 1997).

## The Professions

Increasingly, professions (such as engineering and business) emphasize certain intended outcomes and educational processes. Organizations within these professions help to define the parameters of professional education and the nature of each respective field. Reports from professional associations and business organizations offer recommendations to improve the undergraduate curriculum's effect on student learning. Major leaders from large accounting firms expressed their belief that successful efforts to enhance education require a partnership between faculty and practitioners. In their position paper, these leaders outline the capabilities necessary for practice, including specific communication skills (for example, presenting and defending views formally and informally through written and oral presentations), intellectual skills (for example, using creative problem-solving skills in a consultative process and solving diverse and unstructured problems in unfamiliar environments), and interpersonal skills (for example, working in groups with diverse members to accomplish a task, influencing others, and resolving conflicts) (Arthur Andersen and Company and others, 1989).

Clear statements of intended outcomes are not sufficient to enhance students' abilities and skills. This report by leaders in the accounting profession strongly urges the use of new teaching techniques, in which students learn by actively participating in their education rather than passively listening to lectures. The report's authors particularly emphasize that key skills such as writing must be integrated across the curriculum. They stress that written assignments must be an important, accepted, and natural part of most or all courses. They believe that teaching methods must provide opportunities for students to experience the kinds of work patterns they will encounter in the public accounting profession, which includes working in groups. Therefore, the curriculum should encourage the use of a team approach.

Another recent report states that undergraduates must not learn only science facts but, most importantly, must learn to make informed judgments about technical matters and to solve complex problems by communicating and working in teams (Advisory Committee to the National Science Foundation Directorate for Education and Human Resources, 1996). This report calls for higher expectations in science, math, engineering, and technology. Its authors cite the issue of curricula and classes that emphasize covering the material and acquiring facts, where undergraduates learn material as pieces of information that are disconnected from themselves and from a context that has no meaning to or interest for the students. This report suggests that real or simulated research experiences need to be built into introductory courses so that students discover the importance of certain facts, such as major societal issues or the exploration of new technological opportunities. Innovative courses that succeed for most students seem to have in common a balance between facts and concepts, and they provide a context for the material (Advisory Committee to the National Science Foundation Directorate for Education and Human Resources, 1996). Another engineering report (American Society for Engineering Education, 1994) calls upon engineering colleges to accelerate their aims to incorporate team skills (including collaborative and active learning), communication skills, and leadership. These skills are considered important to prepare individuals to make effective decisions and set policies in professions other than engineering. They also focus upon the need to give both students (including nonmajors) and faculty a greater understanding of engineering's role in society. This group concludes that engineering colleges should be part of "a seamless system that links all of their constituents in education, industry, and the broad public community" (p. 18). The creation of these seamless webs could be important for all professional fields.

## Accreditation

The values and priorities of each profession are reflected in their accreditation standards and guidelines that articulate minimum expectations for the structures, processes, and outcomes of education. In effect, specialized accreditation fosters the development and maintenance of high-quality programs through the creation and implementation of criteria and guidelines for assessing those criteria. In a study of accreditation practices in ten different professional fields, interpersonal communication competence was rated very high by nearly all faculty members (Hagerty and Stark, 1989). Specialized accreditation, regardless of the specific field, sets forth guidelines that seek to promote a curriculum in which undergraduates master the ability to link technical knowledge with appropriate values and attitudes when making complex judgments. These abilities include problem solving, critical thinking, communication and interpersonal skills, professional ethics, and an understanding of the context for professional practice. Exemplary professional education programs "supplement purely technical and conceptual competence with concerns for adaptability, leadership potential, and motivation for continued improvement of the profession and of one's self as a professional" (Stark and Lowther, 1988, p. 22). In the work environment, new employees encounter both familiar and unfamiliar contexts requiring them to use their analytical skills to make difficult decisions.

Regional accrediting organizations require outcomes assessment from their members. These groups require evidence that institutions are attaining their educational purposes. For example, the North Central Association of Colleges and Schools (1994) emphasizes its commitment to the use of assessment in the evaluation and improvement of educational programs. Furthermore, the association expects its affiliated members to regularly submit assessment plans and programs. These plans must show a pattern of evidence that the institution documents the academic achievement of its students (p. 45). North Central outlines the role of general education and expects that such competencies including "reading, writing, speaking, listening, abstract inquiry, critical thinking, and logical reasoning" will be developed by undergraduates (p. 46).

## National Initiatives

The federal government has also stimulated educational reform through numerous initiatives, including its statement of vision entitled Goals 2000. In the winter of 1990, the president and the governors announced several education goals for the nation to be achieved by the year 2000. Goal six, objective five, calls for an increasing number of college graduates who possess advanced abilities to think critically, solve problems, and communicate effectively. The attainment of this goal was envisioned to enable our college graduates to compete in the global economy and exercise the rights and responsibilities of citizenship.

A number of formal initiatives were undertaken to determine how college graduates' abilities and skills could be assessed and to document their cumulative learning as concrete evidence of the nation's progress. The National Education Goals Panel convened four public hearings where individuals testified about the merits and weaknesses regarding the development of a national initiative (Jones, 1993). Subsequently, the National Center for Education Statistics (NCES) sponsored a series of planning workshops where various experts were asked to outline their vision for what should be assessed, the levels of learning that should be expected, and when and how the assessment should be implemented (Corrallo, 1994, 1993). In 1992 and 1994, the NCES contracted three national studies to identify the essential skills that college graduates should master to be effective in the workplace and in society (Jones and others, 1994; Jones, Dougherty, and Fantaske, 1997).

## State-Level Policies and Practices

In the 1980s, many state-level policies from higher education coordinating boards or similar agencies provided an impetus for the implementation and emphasis on assessment at many colleges and universities. Often, these statewide activities were viewed negatively, because the "state made us do it," rather than creating initiatives that were central to change on campus. Assessment in many states was not integral to institutions, and these programs operated as separate projects (McGuiness, 1994). Institutional administrators and faculty tended to view state policies as an intrusion on their academic freedom and institutional autonomy. Such policies were presumed to lead to standardized testing, common measures for all institutions, and lowering standards to a minimum level while "teaching to the test."

Tennessee was the first state to adopt a student assessment policy in 1979; that policy emphasized statewide testing and funding based on the results of assessments. Because this was the first model, many viewed state assessment initiatives as being driven by multiple choice questions on standardized instruments. However, a different model emerged in Virginia in 1985, where institutions had the freedom to select the criteria, methods, and measures for assessment of general education and major fields of study in undergraduate education. Funds were allocated to institutions to support the development of local assessment that reflected the institutions' own missions, student population, and curricula (National Center for Education Statistics, 1996).

In Missouri, a recent initiative, "Funding for Results," seeks to implement performance-funding principles at both the state and campus levels. The Coordinating Board of Higher Education was recently awarded a grant from the Fund for the Improvement of Postsecondary Education to build upon this state initiative. Their main goal is to create a coalition for change that links policy on funding, assessment, and accountability with a program to improve teaching and learning at their campuses (Stein and Fajen, 1995).

The Oregon State System of Higher Education (OSSHE) has articulated an assessment model that seeks to improve "the lives of students, including their retention, learning, and success as well as demonstrate accountability to students and their parents, elected officials, other agencies and employers" (1995, p. 2). They have several campus initiatives under way that link with the overall state framework. Some academic leaders are identifying the skills and dispositions that college graduates should attain and are exploring ways to teach critical thinking more effectively. Other academic leaders have begun to assess student learning particularly in the areas of writing and mathematics. Some institutions have surveyed employers to determine the skills that college graduate need for the workplace.

In Utah, the Regents' Task Force on General Education Assessment has identified key learning criteria that cut across the two- and four-year institutions. Key knowledge and skills in writing, quantitative analysis, and computer and information technology have been discussed by task force subcommittees consisting of faculty in pertinent disciplines from across the state. The commissioner of higher education and other members of the higher education community have recommended reform efforts, particularly in terms of developing an accountable outcome-based system that will establish an education system in which students advance by demonstrating competency rather than by credit hours (National Center for Education Statistics, 1996). Students will demonstrate competency through the use of diverse assessment measures and methods.

Community colleges now conduct required assessment of basic skills for new students and use the results to place students into appropriate coursework or remediation. In Florida, Texas, New Jersey, and Tennessee these processes are direct results of state initiatives and have demonstrated an effectiveness in student retention and performance in coursework in statewide follow-up studies (Ewell, 1993).

In contrast with externally driven statewide policy initiatives, a grass roots approach was undertaken in the state of Washington. Faculty organized the Washington Center (headquartered at The Evergreen State College) as a formal network of faculty across disciplines and administrators who worked together to improve undergraduate education. Through a series of workshops, conferences, and faculty exchanges across the state with both community colleges and universities, the center is designed to enhance faculty development within the classroom and to encourage curriculum reforms. Faculty in different institutions within the state have adopted new approaches to teaching and have created new curricular designs. For example, at Shoreline Community College, faculty have linked composition and content courses to emphasize writing and critical thinking across the curriculum (Smith, 1988). In addition, some studies that have evaluated students' cognitive development in the newly designed coordinated studies programs (at several institutions in Washington) demonstrate that these new programs are effective in developing higher-order thinking (MacGregor, 1987).

There is no predominant model of statewide assessment policies. In fact, no two state policies are exactly the same (Paulson, 1990). Few are grounded in research on assessment (Ewell, 1993). Some were established by statute, others by executive order, and most by action of a state higher education agency or coordinating board. Although these agencies give considerable discretion to the individual institution, they do identify what should be reported, how often, and how the information is to be used.

Although some faculty and university administrators are concerned with external intrusions, these state policies have provided the motivation for many institutions to begin their assessment initiatives. Institutional administrators and state policymakers in Virginia agree that both "the quality and utility of the resulting information has increased markedly (Ewell, 1993, p. 346; Ewell, 1992; Miller, 1991). A majority of the campuses seem willing to continue local assessment regardless of what the state requires (Ewell, 1993). Statewide assessment policies also seem to encourage institutions to discover locally that the results of assessment are useful and that the process is worth sustaining (Ewell, 1993).

Another benefit from external statewide policy actions is that some institutions (in, for example, Colorado and New Jersey) have developed goals and report them in terms of outcomes. In many cases, this goal development process has been perfunctory, but in some cases it has led to substantial and productive dialogue about instructional strategies and the curriculum that might not have taken place (Ewell, 1993). Some states, such as Colorado, have found remarkable overlap in the actual content of the goal statements for their institutions, although each was developed independently (Ewell, 1990). Some dialogues about educational goals and outcomes have taken place among faculty, but such discussions usually do not include employers, policymakers, alumni, nor currently enrolled undergraduates.

Recently, Ewell (1996) completed a national inventory of state-level assessment activities. He found that most states advocate an institution-centered approach, under which colleges develop their own assessment and use their results without common measures across institutions. This decentralized approach encourages institutions to develop assessment plans and expectations that fit their own institutional mission, curriculum, and student populations. Most of these approaches include guidelines for the development of assessment measures but do not require common measures. About 15 percent of the states currently have common undergraduate-outcomes measures under development or already in place (for example, Florida, Texas, and Georgia) (Ewell, 1996). More states are creating linkages with funding initiatives. In 1989, only one state (Tennessee) linked student performance on certain assessment measures within a university with additional funding; today, about thirteen more states are operating funding programs that have ties with student outcomes (Ewell, 1996). Most state-level policymakers who responded to this survey believed that "accountability demands on higher education are more urgent and sharply focused than a decade ago and that current decentralized state-level assessment approaches are inadequate to meet such demands" (p. 13). Ewell summarized a number of issues from the policymakers' perspectives, including the lack of appropriate instruments available to measure critical thinking and communications skills and the need for faculty and the university community to agree about the domains to be assessed.

## Conclusion

Although the 1990s is the second decade of emphasis on educational outcomes by state agencies, accrediting organizations, and the federal government, most faculty still have not seriously considered the assessment of student outcomes (Banta, Lund, Black, and Oblander, 1996). In the Association of American Colleges and Universities' initial stages of work with academic institutions, they found that not a single department of the total fifty-four academic programs involved in their "learning in the major" project (undertaken from 1986 through 1989) had defined goals for student learning in any terms that could usefully guide assessment (Schneider, 1997). Without clear, explicit goals for student outcomes, it is difficult to implement a meaningful assessment plan that will lead to improvements in student learning and in the curriculum.

The external pressures may ultimately influence more faculty and administrators to find ways to raise levels of student learning, reform the curriculum, and restructure how they do business. However, some faculty (without external pressures) are taking responsibility and becoming more active in defining, implementing, and evaluating their plans to determine the quality of student learning at their own respective institutions. Banta, Lund, Black, and Oblander (1996) assembled 165 cases of exemplary assessment practices. Faculty and administrators did implement concrete improvement measures based on their findings. These enhancements included changes in classroom activities to foster student learning of specific outcomes; changes in curricula to address student learning needs discovered in the assessment process; and improvements in the design of exams, assessments of student performance in internships, and the assignment of grades (Banta, Lund, Black, and Oblander, 1996). These campus illustrations serve as useful examples that faculty and administrators should review to find new ideas and methods for creating change at their own campuses. New insights can also be gained from the national and state-level initiatives currently under way and discussed in this chapter.

## References

Advisory Committee to the National Science Foundation Directorate for Education and Human Resources. *Shaping the Future: New Expectations for Undergraduate Education in Science, Mathematics, Engineering, and Technology.* Arlington, Va.: Advisory Committee to the National Science Foundation Directorate for Education and Human Resources, 1996.

American Society for Engineering Education. *Engineering Education for a Changing World.* Washington, D.C.: American Society for Engineering Education, 1994.

Association of American Colleges. *Integrity in the College Curriculum: A Report to the Academic Community.* Washington, D.C.: Association of American Colleges, 1985.

Association of American Colleges and Universities. *Reports from the Fields: Project on Liberal Learning, Study-In-Depth, and the Arts and Sciences Major.* Washington, D.C.: Association of American Colleges and Universities, 1991.

Arthur Andersen and Company, Arthur Young, Coopers and Lybrand, Deloitte Haskins and Sells, Ernst and Whinney, Peat Marwick Main and Company, Price Waterhouse, and Touche Ross. *Perspectives on Education: Capabilities for Success in the Accounting Profession.* New York: Arthur Andersen and Company, Arthur Young, Coopers and Lybrand, Deloitte Haskins and Sells, Ernst and Whinney, Peat Marwick Main and Company, Price Waterhouse, and Touche Ross, 1989.

Banta, T. W., Lund, J. P., Black, K. E., and Oblander, F. W. *Assessment in Practice: Putting Principles to Work on College Campuses.* San Francisco: Jossey-Bass, 1996.

Barabas, C. *Technical Writing in a Corporate Culture: A Study of the Nature of Information.* Norwood, N.J.: Ablex, 1990.

Barber, B. R. *Strong Democracy: Participatory Politics for a New Age.* Berkeley: University of California Press, 1984.

Bloom, A. *Closing of the American Mind.* New York: Simon & Schuster, 1987.

Boyer, E. L., and Kaplan, M. *Educating for Survival.* New Rochelle, N.Y.: Change Magazine Press, 1977.

Boyer, E. L., and Levine, A. *A Quest for Common Learning.* Washington, D.C.: Carnegie Foundation for the Improvement of Teaching, 1981.

Carnegie Foundation for the Advancement of Teaching. *Missions of the College Curriculum: A Contemporary Review with Suggestions.* San Francisco: Jossey-Bass, 1977.

Carnevale, A. P., Gainer, L. J., and Meltzer, A. S. *Workplace Basics: The Essential Skills Employers Want.* San Francisco: Jossey-Bass, 1990.

Cheney, L. V. *50 Hours: A Core Curriculum for College Students.* Washington, D.C.: National Endowment for the Humanities, 1989.

Coates, J. F., Jarratt, J., and Mahaffie, J. B. *Future Work: Seven Critical Forces Reshaping Work and the Work Force in North America.* San Francisco: Jossey-Bass, 1990.

College Placement Council. *Developing the Global Workforce: Institute for Colleges and Corporations.* Bethlehem, Pa.: College Placement Council, 1994.

Corrallo, S. "National Assessment of College Student Learning: A Status Report." *Assessment Update,* 1993, 5 (3), 5, 7, 11.

Corrallo, S. *The National Assessment of College Student Learning: Identification of the Skills to Be Taught, Learned and Assessed: A Report on the Proceedings of the Second Study Design Workshop.* Washington, D.C.: National Center for Education Statistics, 1994.

Education Commission of the States. *Toward Common Ground: Defining and Assuring Quality in Undergraduate Education.* Denver: Education Commission of the States, 1995.

Ewell, P. T. *Assessment and the "New Accountability": A Challenge for Higher Education's Leadership.* Denver: Education Commission of the States, 1990.

Ewell, P. T. "Assessment in Hard Times: A Tale of Two States." *Assessment Update,* 1992, 4 (1), 11–12.

Ewell, P. T. "The Role of States and Accreditors in Shaping Assessment Practice." In T. W. Banta and Associates (eds.), *Making a Difference: Outcomes of a Decade of Assessment in Higher Education.* San Francisco: Jossey-Bass, 1993.

Ewell, P. T. "The Current Pattern of State-Level Assessment: Results of a National Inventory." *Assessment Update,* 1996, 8 (3), 1–2, 12–13, 15.

Glaser, E. "Critical Thinking: Education for Citizenship in a Democracy." *National Forum,* 1985, 65 (1), 24–27.

Hagerty, B.M.K., and Stark, J. S. (1989). "Comparing Educational Accreditation Standards in Selected Fields." *Journal of Higher Education,* 1989, *60* (1), 1–20.

Jones, E. A. *Summary of Public Testimony on Objectives 4 and 5 of Goal 5.* University Park: National Center on Postsecondary Teaching, Learning, and Assessment, The Pennsylvania State University, 1993. (ED 358 775)

Jones, E. A., Dougherty, C., and Fantaske, P. *Essential Skills in Critical Reading and Problem Solving for College Graduates: Perspectives of Faculty, Employers, and Policymakers.* University Park: National Center on Postsecondary Teaching, Learning, and Assessment, The Pennsylvania State University, 1997.

Jones, E. A., Hoffman, S., Melander-Moore, L., Ratcliff, G., Tibbetts, S., and Click, B.A.L. *Essential Skills in Writing, Speech and Listening, and Critical Thinking for College Graduates: Perspectives of Faculty, Employers, and Policymakers.* University Park: National Center on Postsecondary Teaching, Learning, and Assessment, The Pennsylvania State University, 1994.

MacGregor, J. *Intellectual Development of Students in Learning Community Programs 1986–1987.* Olympia: Washington Center for Undergraduate Education, 1987.

McGuinness, A. C., Jr. *A Framework for Evaluating State Policy Rules in Improving Undergraduate Education: Stimulating Long-Term Systemic Change.* Boulder, Colo.: Education Commission of the States, 1994.

Miller, M. A. "Assessment in Trying Times." *Assessment Update,* 1991, *3* (6), 1–5.

Morse, S. W. *Renewing Civic Capacity: Preparing College Students for Service and Citizenship.* ASHE-ERIC Higher Education Report No. 8. Washington, D.C.: School of Education and Human Development, The George Washington University, 1989.

National Center for Education Statistics. *The National Assessment of College Student Learning: State-Level Assessment Activities, A Report of the Proceedings of the Third Study Design Workshop.* Washington, D.C.: National Center for Education Statistics, 1996.

North Central Association of Colleges and Schools. *Handbook of Accreditation: 1994–1996.* Chicago: North Central Association of Colleges and Schools, 1994.

Oregon State System of Higher Education. *Higher Education: Assessment and Accountability.* Eugene: Oregon State System of Higher Education, 1995.

Paulson, C. P. *State Initiatives in Assessment and Outcome Measurement: Tools for Teaching and Learning in the 1990s: Individual State Profiles.* Denver: Education Commission of the States, 1990.

Schneider, C. G. "Reforming Arts and Sciences Majors." In J. G. Gaff and J. L. Ratcliff and Associates (eds.), *The Handbook of the Undergraduate Curriculum: A Comprehensive Guide to Purposes, Structures, Practices, and Change.* San Francisco: Jossey-Bass, 1997.

Smith, B. L. "The Washington Center: A Grassroots Approach to Faculty Development and Curriculum Reform. In J. Kurfiss, L. Hilsen, S. Kahn, M. D. Sorcinelli, and R. Tiberius (eds.), *To Improve the Academy: Resources for Student, Faculty, and Institutional Development,* Vol. 7. POD-New Forums Press, 1987.

Southern Regional Education Board. *Assessing Quality in Higher Education: Policy Actions in the SREB states.* Atlanta, GA: SREB, 1993.

Stark, J. S., and Lowther, M. A. Strengthening the Ties that Bind: *Integrating Undergraduate Liberal and Professional Study.* Ann Arbor: University of Michigan, Professional Preparation Network, 1988.

Stein, R. A., and Fajen, A. L. "Missouri's Funding for Results Initiative." In G. H. Gaither (ed.), *Assessing Performance in an Age of Accountability: Case Studies.* New Directions for Higher Education, no. 91. San Francisco: Jossey-Bass, 1995.

Zemsky, R. *Structure and Coherence: Measuring the Undergraduate Curriculum.* Washington, D.C.: Association of American Colleges and Universities, 1989.

*ELIZABETH A. JONES was the principal investigator and project director of a series of national assessment projects. She is a research associate in the Center for the Study of Higher Education and an assistant professor in the graduate higher education program at The Pennsylvania State University. She is also associate editor of the* Journal of General Education.

*Speaking and listening skills are essential for college graduates. Some skills are basic and important for success in college; others are more advanced and necessary for entry into the workforce.*

# Setting Expectations for Speech Communication and Listening

*Rebecca B. Rubin, Sherwyn P. Morreale*

In the 1960s, educators asked why Johnny couldn't read. In the 1970s, the question was extended to writing and mathematics skills. Educators, administrators, and government policymakers responded to these questions by developing national goals and standards: new expectations for our academic institutions and educational systems (National Education Goals Panel, 1992). Also, *assessment,* the method through which the goals and standards are evaluated, became a popular topic on college campuses and at professional conferences (American Association of Higher Education Assessment Forum, 1992).

Consistent with these trends to document learning outcomes, the original question about Johnny's basic skills was extended to include, "Why can't students speak and listen with competence?" Appropriately, communication professionals have demonstrated increasing concern for communication education in higher education during the past twenty years (Chesebro, 1991). The ability to communicate effectively is now recognized as pivotal to personal satisfaction, academic achievement, and professional success.

We begin this chapter by exploring why speech communication and listening are essential competencies for college graduates. We then describe the nature of communication competence for college students. Next, we outline basic skills necessary for communicating in different situations or contexts. We list some nationally recognized persuading, informing, and relating skills, including both basic and advanced skills for college graduates. We then conclude with a discussion of effective methods for providing instruction in speaking and listening and for assessing students' skills.

## The Importance of Communication

Oral communication competency is essential to a happy and productive life. In fact, oral communication skills make our species unique. It is through communication that we develop and define our sense of self, interact with the environment, and regulate our interactions with others at home, at school, and at work. But our skills are not what they should be. Consider that more than 25 percent of young people (ages eighteen to twenty-four) cannot perform basic communication tasks such as giving clear oral directions (Vangelisti and Daly, 1989). Almost 95 percent of the population reports some degree of anxiety about communicating with another person or in groups (Richmond and McCroskey, 1995). Adults listen at a 25 percent level of efficiency (Berko, Wolvin, and Wolvin, 1995). Most employees show a significant lack of effective speaking and listening skills (DiSalvo, 1980; Hanna, 1978; Henry and Richmond, 1982).

**The Centrality of Talk.** Communication is central to our society. Furthermore, it is essential for academic and professional success. Students write about a book a year and read about a book a month, but they listen as much as a book a day and speak as much as a book a week (Buckley, 1992). Because speaking and listening are integral to students' academic and personal lives, regulating boards and accrediting agencies are mandating that communication skills be included in higher education curricula. They, too, agree that oral communication is central to our society and its economy.

**Communication and Academic and Professional Success.** An array of academic studies and other surveys substantively support McCloskey's suggestion that national efforts be taken to make "talk" central (1994). Competency in speaking and listening repeatedly have been identified as prerequisites to success in school, in the workplace, and in life in general.

Communication skills developed and polished in college are equally important for effective participation in the work world. In many studies and surveys, employers have identified communication abilities as essential for successful work situations (see, for example, Curtis, Winsor, and Stephens, 1989; DiSalvo, Larsen, and Seiler, 1976).

A variety of communication skills also are evident in *What Work Requires of Schools: A SCANS Report for America 2000* (U.S. Department of Labor, 1993). This report identified competencies, skills, and qualities needed for solid job performance. Included in the competencies are interpersonal skills, working on teams, teaching others, leading, negotiating, problem solving, and working well with people from culturally diverse backgrounds. Also included on the list of foundational or important basic skills for effective workers were speaking and listening.

Lastly, several recent surveys and documents also call attention to the importance of communication in education (Berko, 1996). "Given the Circumstances: Teachers Talk About Public Education Today" is a recent study conducted by the Public Agenda Foundation that found that 83 percent of teachers surveyed and 88 percent of the general public felt that students should not be allowed to graduate from high school unless they clearly demonstrate they can speak well. Also, a national study of school evaluation, "Schools of Quality," included "Communication Skills" and "Interpersonal Skills" as goals for student learning. As noted earlier and supported by business and industry professionals, speaking and listening skills are essential for all Americans.

## Achieving Communication Competence

Given the increasing importance of communication skills and the inclusion of speaking and listening in the educational curricula, it is important that the discipline agrees on what communication is and what it entails. Communication researchers seem to agree that competent communication involves motivation, knowledge, and skill.

At a 1995 conference of the Association for Communication Administration, the communication academy reached a consensus on what constitutes the core of the field: "The field of communication focuses on how people use messages to generate meaning within and across various contexts, cultures, channels, and media. It promotes the effective and ethical practice of human communication" (Berko, 1995, p. 12). Given this definition, we can generate a set of elements that constitute the human communication process. These elements help clarify what communication is and determine the scope or domain in which communication operates. *People* encode and decode verbal and nonverbal *symbols,* which are interpreted as *messages* when conveyed intentionally or seen as such, that have some *meaning* for the sender and receiver. A *channel,* or conduit (such as the human voice, a telephone, electronic mail, or radio waves), is required. Communication takes place within a *context,* which shapes the interaction, how messages are interpreted, and how effective the communication act was. Contexts include but are not limited to intrapersonal, interpersonal, small group, public speaking, organizational, mass, and intercultural communication. Communication acts also occur within *cultures.* Like contexts, cultures shape interactions, interpretations, appropriateness, and effectiveness.

Given an understanding of what constitutes communication, the next question relates to the nature of communication competence. Although communication scholars sometimes differ in their focus, most would agree that communication competence involves perceptions of appropriateness and effectiveness (Rubin, 1990). *Appropriateness* is acting in ways that take into account society's rules or norms for the situation. *Effectiveness* is accomplishing one's communication goal. To these, Daly (1994) added several others: involvement and responsiveness, adaptability and flexibility, clarity, efficiency, and politeness. These elements constitute communication competence (Rubin, 1990).

Another useful model of competence, which has been embraced by communication scholars and teachers (Rubin, 1983, 1990; Spitzberg, 1983) as well as by regional and state accreditation agencies (Lopez, 1996), defines competence in terms of learning domains: cognitive (knowledge acquisition), behavioral (skills acquisition), and affective (attitudinal development). *Cognitive competence* involves knowledge of specific facts, principles, and understanding through synthesis and message evaluation. *Behavioral competence* is concerned with psychomotor skills, or the ability to perform certain behaviors based on prior cognitive learning; communicators need to organize their thoughts and communicate them appropriately and effectively to others. *Affective competence* involves positive attitudes and feelings about communicating with others. Speakers must know how to construct competent messages, perform in a way that is seen as competent, and be motivated or predisposed to communicate with others (Daly, 1994).

## Basic Skills for College Graduates

Although knowledge about communication principles and positive attitudes about communication are important, most administrators tend to see the behavioral domain of communication competence as most central to instruction. Skills classes focus on training students to perform better and demonstrate improvement in speaking and listening.

Communication effectiveness is fundamental to learning and is the essence of the teaching-learning process in the classroom. That effectiveness includes speaking or sender skills—the ability to speak out and ask questions and to synthesize one's thoughts verbally to others—and it includes listening or receiver skills—the ability to comprehend and understand spoken messages, lectures, and instructions. Several empirical studies directly correlate oral competency and communication training with academic success (Rubin, Graham, and Mignerey, 1990; Vangelisti and Daly, 1989). But what skills should be taught? Which are basic and which are more advanced?

The Speech Communication Association (SCA) has provided leadership in determining basic standards for both high school and college students. In a document entitled *Speaking, Listening, and Media Literacy Standards for K Through 12 Education* (Speech Communication Association, 1996), communication specialists from across the country identified twenty-three essential skills for effective K–12 speakers, listeners, and media participants. These skills were built upon a previous SCA (1978) document, *SCA Guidelines for Minimal Competencies in Speaking and Listening for High School Graduates.* One college-level study found that all but 1 percent of the students tested could pronounce words acceptably, 10 percent could ask questions effectively, and 16 percent had some articulation difficulties (Rubin, 1982). But over 30 percent of the students could not give accurate directions, 35 percent could not express and defend a point of view, over 27 percent could not listen with understanding to suggestions made to them, about 45 percent could not describe two different opinions, and almost 50 percent could not describe another's viewpoint when it differed from their own. National surveys confirm that young people have extreme difficulty relaying specific information, giving instructions, defending personal opinions, and giving clear oral directions (Vangelisti and Daly, 1989). This research demonstrates that skills once considered basic must be developed before students enter college in that they are necessary for both college and workforce success (Rubin, 1982).

At the 1995 SCA annual convention, another group of educators focused on the undergraduate student canon, or standards for college students. These standards provide the basics of what students should be able to do or know by the time they reach college. Because they are so basic, they are relevant for college as well as beyond. Standards guide curricula by specifying what should be taught. Once general agreement occurs, curricula can be developed to help high schools and colleges fulfill their missions. Another set of basic and more advanced communication skills has already been developed in a national study (Jones, 1994). Groups of faculty, employers, and policymakers completed goals inventories and came to some agreement. Some of the skills are very basic (for example, the skill of structuring messages with introductions, main points, useful transitions, and conclusions).

## Advanced Skills for College Graduates and Beyond

Advanced communication skills involve more than just knowing, doing, or feeling. They are blends of knowledge, skill, and attitude. They also require greater levels of behavioral flexibility or adaptability. For instance, a basic skill such as identifying communication goals at an advanced level becomes *managing multiple communication goals*. This advanced skill requires both identification of the goals and the behavioral component of managing the goals, both of which require adaptability.

More advanced skills also require reasoning and audience analysis. Examples of advanced skills include being able to understand people from other cultures, organizations, or groups and adapting messages to the demands of the situation or context (Jones, 1994); identifying and adapting to changes in audience characteristics; incorporating language that captures and maintains audience interest; identifying and managing misunderstandings; demonstrating credibility, competence, and comfort with information; and showing attentiveness through nonverbal and verbal behaviors. These skills require greater emphasis on creating appropriate and effective messages, two main components of competence. College graduates also need to refine their listening skills; they need to identify important issues or problems, draw conclusions, and understand others to better manage conflict and empathize with their colleagues. Jones concluded that "advanced skills in both writing and speech communication require the development of reasoning skills" (p. 38). Speech communication educators have long been teaching reasoning skills, because they realized that even basic communication skills require sound reasoning. Here are some of the more advanced skills, again supported by the survey of faculty, employers, and policy makers (Jones, 1994):

- Incorporate information from a variety of sources to support message.
- Identify and use appropriate statistics to support the message.
- Use motivational appeals that build on audience values, expectations, and needs.
- Develop messages that influence attitudes, beliefs, and actions.
- Manage and resolve group conflicts effectively.
- Approach confidently and engage in conversation with new people in new settings.
- Negotiate effectively.
- Allow others to express different views and attempt to understand them.
- Effectively assert themselves while respecting others' rights.
- Understand and value differences in communication styles.
- Motivate others to participate and work effectively as a team.
- Understand and implement different methods of building group consensus.
- Set and manage realistic agendas.
- Lead meetings effectively.

As Harris and Cronen (1979) explained, employees with minimal levels of competence can perform the tasks required of them; higher levels of competence are achieved when employees know why they are acting in this way (because they know the goals of the organization) and can see how these actions fit into the organization's goals vis-à-vis society. We would expect most beginning college students to have very basic skill levels, which are then refined and developed throughout the college experience via courses or other instructional methods. By the time they graduate, college students should have mastered advanced skills—those needed to enter the workforce—and should be prepared for even higher levels of communication competence once they learn their organization's goals.

## Effective Methods of Instruction and Assessment

If faculty and administrators agree with the premise that oral communication skills are important for college graduates, then policy decisions need to be made. How should speech communication and listening be incorporated into the college curriculum? Should a basic communication course be required of all graduates, and, if so, what should be taught in the course? What other approaches or methods of communication instruction might be effective and represent viable options? What assessment methods will ensure that the institution's graduates are orally competent? As with the nature of communication competency, teachers and administrators active in this field have been examining these questions.

**Courses.** A single learning event—such as a public speaking, small group, or interpersonal communication course—can be helpful in developing some degree of communication competency. Based on these three communication contexts, another option is the hybrid, or basic, course in communication. Typically, the basic communication course (often termed *fundamentals*) includes three units that focus on the three contexts: interpersonal, small group, and public speaking. However, a single communication course, no matter how good it is, may be insufficient to develop advanced competency and skills needed by college students to succeed beyond college. Students need exposure to cognitive information and practice in using communication skills in a variety of situations to achieve advanced competency levels.

Communication skills can best be taught and assessed according to the specific context in which they occur: interpersonal skills, group skills, and public speaking. Interpersonal communication involves only two people. Social conversation, interviewing, and conflict management skills can be studied within the interpersonal dyad. Group communication involves three to eight people; group communicators need group process, mediation, and task skills along with interpersonal skills. Public communication involves communication from one to many. Therefore, courses focusing on these areas provide a logical method of instruction and assessment.

**Instruction Across the Curriculum.** An integrated and varied approach, referred to in the literature as communication across the curriculum, may support a more comprehensive experience in communication for undergraduates (Cronin and Grice, 1993; Morreale, Shockley-Zalabak, and Whitney, 1993). This model has been used extensively on college campuses to provide additional opportunities for writing experience in content-specific areas. Similar programs for oral communication skills are also prevalent and efficient methods of reinforcing basic skills.

A program in communication across the curriculum is similar in some ways to writing across the curriculum. Faculty from noncommunication disciplines are encouraged to include oral communication activities in existing courses. The communication department and faculty may provide support and training to facilitate that process and to enhance the quality of the communication experience for the student. The across-the-curriculum program could include communication instruction and components in a wide selection of noncommunication courses. In these communication-intensive courses, students could be introduced by communication faculty to communication processes and skills as part of their discipline-specific coursework. Additionally, oral communication components could be included in entry-level freshman orientation courses and in exit-level senior capstone courses. In combination with a required communication course, such a varied and comprehensive approach would support the goals of achieving students' incremental development of communication skills and graduating a more orally competent workforce.

**Assessment.** Although this was not the case twenty years ago, today, many instruments exist for assessing students' communication skills. The development of assessment instruments seemed to follow trends in curriculum development. Traditional classroom assessments, such as exams, surveys, or tests, have been supplemented with newer, more applied assessments such as exit interviews, capstone courses, and portfolios (Arneson, 1994). These measures provide a qualitative view of outcomes assessment.

Numerous quantitative large-scale instruments have been developed for use in classrooms also. Morreale and Backlund (1996) have edited a volume summarizing these instruments, entitled *Large Scale Assessment of Oral Communication, Edition Two: Kindergarten Through Grade 12, and Higher Education.* It includes overall reviews of speaking and listening instruments and individual summaries of those available for general use. One instrument that provides an assessment of basic college-level skills is the *Communication Competency Assessment Instrument* (Rubin, 1994).

Instruments assessing more specific skills also exist for either classroom or outcomes assessment. For example, valid and reliable measures of listening ability, interpersonal skills, group communication skills, public speaking ability, cognitive skills, and intercultural communication competence are available (Morreale and Backlund, 1996; Rubin, Palmgreen, and Sypher, 1994; Spitzberg and Cupach, 1989). Three representative rating scales for specific skills are: the *Conversational Skills Rating Scale* (Spitzberg, 1994), the *Competent Group Communicator* (Beebe, Barge, and McCormick, 1994), and *The Competent Speaker* (Morreale, Moore, Taylor, Surges-Tatum, and Hulbert-Johnson, 1993).

**Guidelines for Assessing Oral Communication.** Some universities have developed comprehensive programs for assessment to ensure students' incremental acquisition of necessary communication skills and graduates' achievement of a satisfactory degree of communication competency (Morreale and Brooks, 1994). For example, since the 1970s, Alverno College has been using qualitative techniques to assess its students' communication skills throughout the college experience (Wulff, 1994). And The University of Colorado at Colorado Springs has developed a fairly comprehensive assessment program using mostly quantitative measures (Shockley-Zalabak and Hulbert-Johnson, 1994). These programs help facilitate student learning, direct course content and instruction, and provide measures of learning outcomes.

## Conclusions

Basic communication skills should be required for all college students. Additional across-the-curriculum programs and advanced skills classes are needed to be sure that entry-level workers of the future can deal with the demands of the future. Communication is a complicated area, encompassing many skills. Efforts to communicate must be seen as appropriate by others and must also work. Communicators must be able to understand the audience and situation and adapt to them. Their communication, then, should be clear and efficient, and they should be seen as involved and polite. Competent communication requires knowledge, skill, and motivation. Colleges can teach basic communication principles to enhance knowledge, can find classroom and extracurricular activities to hone skills, and can help students develop positive attitudes and feelings about communicating with others. Communication across the curriculum will help students refine their basic skills, and numerous assessment instruments can help determine if basic skills have been developed.

Advanced skills, however, require combinations of knowledge, skills, and attitude; these skills could be taught in advanced classes, perhaps taught jointly by both major discipline and communication faculty. These capstone courses could focus on communication situations and contexts within each discipline and would allow students to explore optional behaviors, based on knowledge of what would be appropriate and effective in that context. Assessment instruments, perhaps administered in campus assessment centers, must be developed to measure students' preparedness for workplace communication. These would help students understand skill development still needed to function effectively in society.

## References

American Association of Higher Education Assessment Forum. *The Principles of Good Practice for Assessing Student Learning.* Washington, D.C.: American Association of Higher Education Assessment Forum, 1992.

Arneson, P. "Assessing Communication Competence Through Portfolios, Scoring Rubrics, and Personal Interviews." In S. Morreale and M. Brooks (eds.), *1994 SCA Summer Conference Proceedings and Prepared Remarks: Assessing College Student Competency in Speech Communication.* Annandale, Va.: Speech Communication Association, 1994.

Beebe, S. A., Barge, J. K., and McCormick, C. "The Competent Group Communicator." In S. Morreale and M. Brooks (eds.), *1994 SCA Summer Conference Proceedings and Prepared Remarks: Assessing College Student Competency in Speech Communication.* Annandale, Va.: Speech Communication Association, 1994.

Berko, R. "ACA Conference Defines the Field." *Spectra,* 1995, *31* (10), 12.

Berko, R. "Speaking, Listening Promoted in Study Documents." *Spectra,* 1996, *32* (6), 12.

Berko, R., Wolvin, A., and Wolvin, D. *Communicating: A Social and Career Focus.* (6th ed.) Boston: Houghton Mifflin, 1995.

Buckley, M. F. "Focus on Research: We Listen a Book a Day; We Speak a Book a Week: Learning from Walter Loban." *Language Arts,* 1992, *69,* 622–626.

Chesebro, J. "Oral Communication Competency and Assessment as a Component of College and University Accreditation." *The Carolinas' Speech Communication Annual,* 1991, *7,* 7–22.

Cronin, M. W., and Grice, G. L. "A Comparative Analysis of Training Models Versus Consulting/Training Models for Implementing Oral Communication Across the Curriculum." *Communication Education,* 1993, *42,* 1–9.

Curtis, D. B., Winsor, J. L., and Stephens, R. D. "National Preferences in Business and Communication Education." *Communication Education,* 1989, *38,* 6–14.

Daly, J. A. "Assessing Speaking and Listening: Preliminary Considerations for a National Assessment." In S. Morreale and M. Brooks (eds.), *1994 SCA Summer Conference Proceedings and Prepared Remarks: Assessing College Student Competency in Speech Communication.* Annandale, Va.: Speech Communication Association, 1994.

DiSalvo, V. S. "A Summary of Current Research Identifying Communication Skills in Various Organizational Contexts." *Communication Education,* 1980, *29,* 283–290.

DiSalvo, V., Larsen, D. C., and Seiler, W. J. "Communication Skills Needed by Persons in Business Organizations." *Communication Education,* 1976, *25,* 269–275.

Hanna, M. S. "Speech Communication Training Needs in the Business Community." *Central States Speech Journal,* 1978, *29,* 163–172.

Harris, L., and Cronen, V. E. "A Rules-Based Model for the Analysis and Evaluation of Organizational Communication." *Communication Quarterly,* 1979, 27 (1), 12–28.

Henry, J. J., and Richmond, S. U. *Basic Skills in the United States Work Force.* New York: Center for Public Resources, 1982.

Jones, E. A. *Essential Skills in Writing, Speech and Listening, and Critical Thinking for College Graduates: Perspectives of Faculty, Employers, and Policymakers.* University Park: National Center for Postsecondary Teaching, Learning, and Assessment, The Pennsylvania State University, 1994.

Lopez, C. L. *Opportunities for Improvement: Advice from Consultant-Evaluators on Programs to Assess Student Learning.* Chicago: North Central Accreditation Commission on Institutions of Higher Education, 1996.

McCloskey, D. "The Neglected Economics of Talk." *Planning For Higher Education,* 1994, *22,* 11–16.

Morreale, S. P., and Backlund, P. M. (eds.). *Large Scale Assessment of Oral Communication: K-12 and Higher Education.* Annandale, Va.: Speech Communication Association, 1996.

Morreale, S., and Brooks, M. (eds.). *1994 SCA Summer Conference Proceedings and Prepared Remarks: Assessing College Student Competency in Speech Communication.* Annandale, Va.: Speech Communication Association, 1994.

Morreale, S. P., Moore, M., Taylor, P., Surges-Tatum, D., and Hulbert-Johnson, R. *The Competent Speaker.* Annandale, Va.: Speech Communication Association, 1993.

Morreale, S., Shockley-Zalabak, P., and Whitney, P. "The Center for Excellence in Oral Communication: Integrating Communication Across-the-Curriculum." *Communication Education,* 1993, 42, 10–21.

National Education Goals Panel. *Executive Summary: The National Education Goals Report: Building a Nation of Learners.* Washington D.C.: National Education Goals Panel, 1992.

Richmond, V. P., and McCroskey, J. C. *Communication: Apprehension, Avoidance, and Effectiveness.* Scottsdale, Ariz.: Gorusch Scarisbrick, 1995.

Rubin, R. B. "Assessing Speaking and Listening Competence at the College Level: The Communication Competency Assessment Instrument." *Communication Education,* 1982, *31,* 19–32.

Rubin, R. B. "Conclusions." In R. B. Rubin (ed.), *Improving Speaking and Listening Skills.* New Directions for College Learning Assistance, no. 12. San Francisco: Jossey-Bass, 1983.

Rubin, R. B. "Communication Competence." In G. M. Phillips and J. T. Wood (eds.), *Speech Communication: Essays to Commemorate the 75th Anniversary of the Speech Communication Association.* Carbondale: Southern Illinois University Press, 1990.

Rubin, R. B. *Communication Competency Assessment Instrument* (Rev. ed.). New Orleans: Spectra Inc., 1994.

Rubin, R. B., Graham, E. E., and Mignerey, J. "A Longitudinal Study of College Students' Communication Competence." *Communication Education,* 1990, *38,* 1–14.

Rubin, R. B., Palmgreen, P., and Sypher, H. (eds.). *Communication Research Measures: Sourcebook.* New York: Guilford Press, 1994.

Shockley-Zalabak, P., and Hulbert-Johnson, R. "Assessment at the University of Colorado at Colorado Springs: The Center for Excellence in Oral Communication." In S. Morreale and M. Brooks (eds.), *1994 SCA Summer Conference Proceedings and Prepared Remarks: Assessing College Student Competency in Speech Communication.* Annandale, Va.: Speech Communication Association, 1994.

Speech Communication Association. *SCA Guidelines for Minimal Competencies in Speaking and Listening for High School Graduates.* Annandale, Va.: Speech Communication Association, 1978.

Speech Communication Association. *Speaking, Listening, and Media Literacy Standards for K through 12 Education.* Annandale, Va.: Speech Communication Association, 1996.

Spitzberg, B. H. "Communication Competence as Knowledge, Skill, and Impression." *Communication Education*, 1983, *32*, 323–329.

Spitzberg, B. H. "Instructional Assessment of Interpersonal Competence: The Conversational Skills Rating Scale." In S. Morreale and M. Brooks (eds.), *1994 SCA Summer Conference Proceedings and Prepared Remarks: Assessing College Student Competency in Speech Communication*. Annandale, Va.: Speech Communication Association, 1994.

Spitzberg, B. H., and Cupach, W. R. *Handbook of Interpersonal Competence Research*. New York: Springer-Verlag, 1989.

U.S. Department of Labor. 1993. *What Work Requires of Schools: A SCANS Report for America 2000*. Washington, D.C.

Vangelisti, A. L., and Daly, J. A. "Correlates of Speaking Skills in the United States: A National Assessment." *Communication Education*, 1989, *38*, 132–143.

Wulff, S. "To Sit Down Beside: Assessment and Communication Competence at Alverno College." In S. Morreale and M. Brooks (eds.), *1994 SCA Summer Conference Proceedings and Prepared Remarks: Assessing College Student Competency in Speech Communication*. Annandale, Va.: Speech Communication Association, 1994.

*SHERWYN P. MORREALE is associate director of the Speech Communication Association. She is former director of the Center for Excellence in Oral Communication at the University of Colorado at Colorado Springs. Dr. Morreale is the current chair of the Speech Communication Association's Committee on Assessment and Testing.*

*REBECCA B. RUBIN is Professor of Communication Studies and Director of the Communication Research Center at Kent State University. Dr. Rubin is past chair of the Speech Communication Association's Committee on Assessment and Testing.*

*The essential writing skills important to employers and faculty must be related to the various approaches to teaching writing.*

# Educating Students to Write Effectively

*Benjamin A. L. Click III*

Christine Barabas identifies "two recent and related developments in the research and teaching of writing [that] are beginning to have significant effects" on the discipline of rhetoric and composition: "the growing interest being shown in real-world writing (or what academicians call 'nonacademic' writing and . . . the increased importance being attached to the particular contexts within which texts are written, read, and used" (1990, p. xix). Much empirical study, scholarship about writing in the workplace, and discussion among academicians support Barabas's forecast.

In 1985, Paul Anderson reviewed fifty surveys that investigated the kinds of writing that take place in the workplace (pp. 3–83). The most recent edition of *The Bedford Bibliography for Teachers of Writing* (Bizzell and Herzberg, 1996), a selective bibliography, has an entire section on writing in the workplace, with nineteen entries (the previous edition, 1991, contained no such section). Noting the quadrupling in the last five years of graduate programs in technical and professional communications, the *ATTW Bulletin* (a publication of the Association of Teachers of Technical Writing) published an "interchange" between top technical writing scholars in which they offered "observations about job prospects (in technical writing) for Ph.D.s and the implications for graduate programs" (Brown, Selfe, and Selzer, 1994, p. 5). Clearly, the academic community is concerned with its link to "real-world" writing.

Still, not enough is known about real-world writing. As Barabas notes, "Until recently, the study and teaching of writing have focused primarily upon one type of writing: academic writing, especially the writing that students do in school" (1990, p. 3). In fact, faculty in all disciplines, policymakers in higher education, and campus administrators are beginning to recognize the importance of writing for improving not only communication skills but also analytical abilities, critical inquiry, and knowledge construction and retention. The academic view of writing instruction in the last twenty-five years has focused on the processes of writing (as opposed to the product view of writing) in the hope of developing lifelong learning skills in students. But employers look for graduates who are able to produce high-quality products, and citizens look for tangible ways to cope with and often change their communities. So what approaches do educators in colleges and universities employ to teach students to write effectively? What are the essential writing skills that college graduates should possess to be adequately prepared as employees in the workforce and as citizens in society? What are the implications of such practices for colleges and universities, which strive to accommodate the writing needs of the workforce while maintaining the ideals of a strong liberal education for their students? And how might social, cultural, financial, and technological factors influence these essential writing skills and how they are taught?

For a more detailed understanding of trends and practices in the field of rhetoric and composition than will be provided by this chapter, several bibliographies (many of them with very good annotations) exist that would be useful to academic administrators, deans, department chairs, and members on general education or curriculum development committees: Bizzell and Herzberg (1996), Hillocks (1986); Hawisher and Selfe (1995); Larson (1988); Moran and Lunsford (1984); and Tate (1987). In addition, the Educational Resources Information Center and the Clearinghouse on Reading and Communication Skills (ERIC/RCS), sponsored by the National Council of Teachers of English (NCTE), maintains a computer database of materials, including abstracts of articles on rhetoric and composition. Two other sources offer readable interpretations of the main branches of composition scholarship: McClelland and Donovan's *Perspectives on Research and Scholarship in Composition* (1985) and Faigley's "Competing Theories of Process: A Critique and a Proposal" (1986).

## Three Approaches to Teaching Writing: Expressive, Cognitive, and Social

For the last twenty-five years, the emphasis in writing instruction has been on the composing process (Cooper, 1986; Emig, 1971; Faigley, 1986; Flower and Hayes, 1981; Flower, Wallace, Norris, and Burnett, 1994; Penrose and Sitko, 1993; Perl, 1994; Rose, 1985; Tobin and Newkirk, 1994). Contrasted with the product view of writing, which "emphasizes the structural features of texts," the process view "emphasizes the act of composing itself" (Barabas, 1990, pp. 28, 38). The writing as process movement "reemphasized . . . pre-writing stages, those that precede production of a finished piece of work" (Bizzell and Herzberg, 1996, p. 8). In general, the entire writing process has been identified in three basic stages (each of which has been referred to by many names): *pre-writing, writing,* and *rewriting,* sometimes called planning, drafting, and revision. But the value of the process model is its recursive nature—the idea that each stage is interrelated to all the stages. Writers often do all three stages simultaneously. In order to understand the writing skills that college graduates need to possess for success in the workplace and in society, I will briefly cover the major approaches to teaching the composing process: *expressive, cognitive,* and *social.*

**Expressive.** Expressive theory promotes writing instruction that emphasizes "the self-expressive uses of language, assisting students in shaping their ideas through writing" (Bizzell and Herzberg, 1991, p. 4). Its many proponents include Ken Macrorie (1968), William Coles (1969), Donald Steward (1969), Peter Elbow (1973), Donald Murray (1978), Ann Berthoff (1982), and C. H. Knoblauch and Lil Brannon (1984). Students engage in pre-writing activities such as freewriting (also called automatic writing, babbling, and jabbering exercises; see Elbow, 1973, and Macrorie, 1968) or answering a set of questions in order to help them find a topic and revise and narrow it to a manageable thesis or claim. These exercises can also assist students in developing their own tone and writing style. The pedagogical practices that accompany this theory include high interaction among teacher and students in which the teacher assumes the role of coach rather than the role of authority figure.

The focus of expressive theory is on helping students discover what they feel and know. This focus can help promote an awareness and understanding of cultural diversity that is valued in higher education and in the workforce. If students are encouraged to find their own voice through exercises such as freewriting, they are free to explore and reflect upon their cultural, racial, and ethnic differences with other students and, in turn, may be more tolerant and even accepting of those differences. This feature of expressive theory is particularly important because the workforce and society are increasingly more global.

**Cognitive.** The cognitive theory of composing was influenced by cognitive psychology and psycholinguistics. It investigates the cognitive activities involved in the composing process. It supports the idea that composing is what goes on in the writer's mind and is then recorded in writing. Emig's (1971) experiment revealed that students compose in two modes: *reflexive* (in which the student is concerned with expressing his or her feelings and personal experiences, using an informal writing style) and *extensive* (in which the student is concerned with conveying information in a formal style with the teacher as the primary audience). Emig's study was influential for its conception of composing as a process. Her approach to understanding how writing unfolds led to more empirical studies based on observations of working writers in composition research. Flower and Hayes's (1981) use of "protocol analysis" is one such example.

In the protocol analysis work, writers orally describe their choices while writing a composition. Then the researchers analyze the composition and the descriptions to understand the cognitive nature of the writers' composing process. Flower and Hayes discovered that the composing process is not linear but, rather, hierarchical and recursive. Other empirically based work followed Emig and Flower and Hayes. Nancy Sommers (1980), in her article, "Revision Strategies of Student Writers and Experienced Adult Writers," noted that student writers focus their revisions on surface-level matters such as choosing better words, correcting punctuation, and eliminating repetition, whereas experienced adult writers focus on global concerns of the text—how to better accommodate the audience and more effectively render the argument by adding and deleting material and rearranging sentences and paragraphs.

Students who are non-native English speakers severely test the claims of cognitive theory, however. Although they may be poor writers of standard English, they do not necessarily possess poor cognitive abilities. Rather, these students are linguistically and culturally diverse. As a result of this understanding, the Conference on College Composition and Communication passed a resolution in 1974 concerning students' rights to their own languages. The issue of a standard language is still being debated in state and national forums—for example, in California's recent bill to make English the official language of that state.

**Social.**  Although cognitive theory can offer teachers an understanding of how cognitive processes influence the writing process for individuals, there are also influences within the social contexts in which writers write. Flower's recent book, *The Construction of Negotiated Meaning: A Social Cognitive Theory of Writing* (1994), explores the relationship between writers' strategic processes and social context. Her work offers insight on how increasingly diverse classroom populations learn to write effectively in the workplace and in other nonacademic settings. The proponents of the social nature of writing believe that college students learn to write in reader-based prose of the academic societies they wish to join. They learn to become constituents of those societies. In order to expose students to the notion of the social perspective of writing, teachers turn naturally to collaborative learning because it models social contexts within the classroom.

Collaborative learning practices include peer reviews in writing workshops, small group discussion, descriptive outlines written by peers on rough drafts, and other interactive activities. All of these activities offer students a social context (a place to converse) among their peers (both knowledgeable of and unfamiliar with specific academic and nonacademic fields) who are already members of several communities. In group work individuals strive for consensus as to what constitutes knowledge in a particular community. The work of Kenneth Bruffee (1984, 1986) is especially useful in understanding the social view of writing and collaborative learning. Another good guide to collaborative learning in general is *Collaborative Learning: A Sourcebook for Higher Education* (1992), published by the National Center on Postsecondary Teaching, Learning, and Assessment. This sourcebook defines and describes collaborative learning, discusses its history and where it is used, and includes sections on developing collaborative learning exercises and assessing the effects of collaborative learning.

The importance of the social view of writing cannot be underestimated, particularly when employers consistently seek college graduates who can work collaboratively. Companies use project teams in which progress reports, feasibility studies, year-end market analysis reports, and organizational instructions are written collaboratively. Modeling similar social contexts in the college writing classroom (and any classroom for that matter) makes great sense and has practical as well as academic value. Couture and others (1985) describe the process they implemented at Wayne State, "by which a university can collaborate with business and industry to improve research and curriculum development in professional writing" (p. 392).

These three approaches affect the writing process and its various stages. As cognitive theory identified, that process is not linear but recursive. Thus, whereas expressivist practices such as freewriting may help students generate topics of importance in the pre-writing stage, they may also be employed in the drafting and revision stages to help develop lines of argument or develop a particular writing style. The cognitive approach can offer teachers a means to explore the stages of how a technical document is drafted in a large company, and collaborative exercises can model how the revision of such a technical document may evolve in team projects. All three approaches offer valuable theoretical and practical support to faculty who incorporate writing into their courses and who value the process of writing for its recursive nature and versatility.

## Specific Skills to Be Learned and to Be Taught

Jones and others (1994) developed a writing goals inventory for a national study to identify the writing skills that college graduates need. This instrument listed specific writing skills under a general writing framework. Faculty, employers, and policymakers in higher education were asked to rate the importance of specific writing skills for work and citizenship. The highlighted results of that research will serve to examine the essential writing skills that college graduates should possess to be effective employees and citizens.

**Where Faculty, Employers, and Policymakers Agree About Writing Skills.** As we might assume, faculty in different disciplines and researchers rated many of the skills high in importance. The general skills areas that received the highest percentage of agreement were awareness and knowledge of audience, purpose for writing, organizing, features of written products, and written products.

When composition studies (Bitzer, 1968; Connors, Ede, and Lunsford, 1984; Corbett, 1990; Crowley, 1994) began to reexamine classical rhetoric and apply its theories and practices of public oration to the teaching of writing, being aware of audience attitude, value, knowledge, and belief and understanding the purposes for writing became important features in the writing classroom and in writing assignments.

Students were taught that most writing (especially real-world writing) does not take place in a vacuum—all writing occasions have a rhetorical situation. Bitzer (1968) defines the rhetorical situation "as a complex of persons, events, objects, and relations presenting an actual or potential exigence which can be completely or partially removed if discourse, introduced into the situation, can so constrain human decision or action as to bring about the significant modification of the exigence" (p. 6). In simpler terms, something gives cause for the writing occasion, a particular or general audience is addressed, and the written document serves one or more purposes. Faculty, employers, and policymakers rated the three features (audience, purpose, and organization) of the rhetorical situation discussed earlier as very important.

In addition, college graduates no longer should leave their institutions with only the knowledge of how to write academic prose for the teacher. While helping students identify real audiences is a generally accepted teaching practice, scholarship on audience reveals that it is far from unproblematic—in either theory or practice. Ede and Lunsford (1984) reveal significant differences between an audience addressed (a real audience) and an audience invoked (a fictional audience created by signals given in the text) (see also Ong, 1975). Elbow (1987) suggests that sometimes it is better not to think of the audience, because some audiences inhibit the writing process or intimidate the writer.

More specifically, a national study indicated that "college graduates should be able to consider how an audience will use a particular document, choose words that their audience can comprehend, and understand the relationship between the audience and the subject material" (Jones and others, 1994, p. 37). However, some employers saw addressing audiences whose backgrounds in the topic vary widely and defining multiple anticipated audiences as more advanced skills—ones that new employees do not possess when they enter the workforce. Thus, there is a consistency between faculty, employer, and policymaker and "the previous frameworks of writing that stress the importance of college graduates' abilities to develop a representation of the potential readers of a text (Faigley, Cherry, Jolliffe, and Skinner, 1985; Flower and Hayes, 1980, Odell and Goswami, 1985; Sommers, 1980)" (Jones and others, 1994, p. 76).

College graduates should no longer leave college without being able to understand the purposes of general and particular writing situations. They should also be able to effectively organize their discourses. Important to both educators and employers are the cognitive processes that Flower and Hayes (1981) describe, "[in] which a writer uses a goal to generate ideas, then consolidates those ideas and uses them to revise or regenerate new, more complex goals" (p. 386). Moreover, in generating goals, writers reduce the number of constraints that confront them when they compose (Flower and Hayes, 1980). Booth (1963); Bitzer (1968); Faigley, Cherry, Jolliffe, and Skinner (1985), and others recognize the relationship between audience awareness, subject knowledge, writer persona, and purpose. Under the general skills area of purpose for writing, the three stakeholder groups agreed on four specific skills: the ability to state purposes to audiences, to use vocabulary appropriate to subject and purposes, to arrange words within sentences to fit intended purposes and audiences, and to make appropriate use of creative techniques of humor and eloquence when approaching a writing task (Jones and others, p. 43). As might be expected, faculty rated significantly higher than did policymakers the ability to be aware of multiple purposes and goals (p.43).

In addition to audience awareness, understanding the purposes of a particular writing situation aids in the effective organization of a text's argument. Students should develop the means for creating coherence among words, sentences, and whole sections of writing and view those means and techniques as options from which to chose. Textbooks such as *The Writer's Options* (Daiker, Kerek, Morenberg, and Sommers, 1994), *Style: Ten Lessons in Clarity and Grace* (Williams, 1995), and *Rhetorical Grammar: Grammatical Choices, Rhetorical Effects* (Kolln, 1991) emphasize the rhetorical nature of writing as one of the options governed by audience and purpose. Even punctuation is a rhetorical tool, according to Dawkins (1995). However, Eden and Mitchell (1986) call attention to how admired professional writing differs from the kind of writing prescribed by textbooks, which offer set organizational patterns and rules such as the use of topic sentences. They suggest teaching reader-oriented paragraphing. Fleckenstein asserts that coherence is difficult to teach because it is as much a "reader-based phenomenon as it is a writer-based creation" (1992, p. 82).

**Where Faculty, Employers, and Policymakers Disagree About Writing Skills.** As one would expect, the quality of the final product is important to employers, as evinced by the high rating of skills listed under the general skills areas of features of the written product and producing written products. Specific skills such as the ability to use correct grammar, syntax, punctuation, and spelling; language that the audience understands; and concise language rated highly among all three groups. However, under the general skills areas of features of the written products and different types of documents, there were significant disagreements about specific skills. For example, "employers rate the importance of using visual aids, tables, and graphs as significantly more important than faculty" (Jones and others, 1994, p. 79). Employers offered the following supporting comments about the importance of visual aids: "backbone of the presentation," "extremely important in the business world—sometimes the difference between good and great," "modern communications require the use of these tools," and "critical because this also implies that you know what your audience likes *and* you use it" (pp. 67–68).

The importance of graphic communication is something faculty who emphasize writing need to be more aware of, especially with the growth of electronic communications: television, video, e-mail, and the Internet. Popular text sources such as newspapers and magazines and even academic journals rely more and more on graphic representation to convey meaning.

The general writing skills areas that received the highest percentage of disagreement were the following: pre-writing activities and collaboration. Specifically, analyzing experiences to provide ideas for writing, creating ideas, and retrieving material from memory were not considered as important as other skills by employers. It is the organizational context (specific job responsibilities for new hires and assigned writing tasks) that may render these skills less important to employers. Similarly, although employers and policymakers view collaboration as an important part of some positions within an organization, they "emphasized that collaboration was not expected or realistic due to the nature of an individual's job responsibilities" (Jones and others, 1994, p. 79).

Although the ability to write collaboratively is a valued skill in general, employers differed from faculty and policymakers in three specific collaborative writing skills: critiquing others' drafts, negotiating critiques of one's writing from others, and writing documents for someone else's signature. Faculty saw critiquing others' work as "excellent training" and a means to improve "critical thinking skills" and valued negotiating critiques because doing so "allows the writer to see that writing is a 'product' and so possibly removes oneself from the personal vulnerability" (Jones and others, 1994, pp. 62–63). Although faculty commented that writing for someone else's signature was a "narrow specialization," "a specific skill for a secretarial course" that "seems dishonest," employers and policymakers remarked that "this is what entry-level people often must do—and do so without embarrassment to the 'signer'" (p. 62). Faculty, policymakers, and employers all valued the skill of collaborating with others during reading and writing in a given situation.

The nature of collaboration is such that one can learn from others' knowledge and expertise. As the survey results indicate, academia and business have not reached total consensus on what collaboration means. However, some university communities (Wayne State, for example) have established links between their professional writing programs and industry. Couture and others (1985) offer guidelines for establishing a collaborative team (pp. 393–394).

## Institutional Structures to Support Writing Initiatives, Publication Resources, and Technology

There are various means to assist students in acquiring the skills that are discussed in the previous section. Many of these means (academic services and curriculum development, for example) depend on sufficient staffing and funding. Some require additional resources such as hardware and software for useful technology.

Writing centers have been around since the 1930s, but the administration of today's writing centers and the tutoring that takes place in them have changed. Some centers are part of an institutional learning center, some are housed in individual departments and used for those disciplines only, and some are housed in English departments. More and more centers effectively employ student help in the form of peer tutoring. Tutoring in general gives students one-on-one help and serves as an extension to classroom instruction. Several writing centers are on-line and may be accessed through a campus computer network or the Internet (Hult and Kinkead, 1995). There is much available on writing center theory, practice, and administration (Harris, 1986, 1995; Mullin and Wallace, 1994; Murphy and Law, 1995; Olson, 1984).

Real-world writing needs are being addressed by the writing across the curriculum (WAC) movement and department course offerings. Both promote the importance of writing as an essential skill for communication, knowledge construction and retention, analytical reasoning, and critical thinking. In addition, both approach writing from two broad concepts: "writing to learn" (writing is used in courses to help learn discipline-specific material and concepts) and "learning to write" (students learn to write as members of a specific discipline). More and more administrators are asking teachers to incorporate writing across the curriculum in their introductory writing courses (Blalock, 1994). In addition, various writing courses complement the notion that real-world writing is important in the academic setting: technical writing, business writing, writing in the social sciences, and so on. Useful sources for understanding WAC and its recent development are Anson, Schwiebert, and Williamson (1993), Bizzell and Herzberg (1986), Blalock (1994), and Maimon (1997). Elaine Maimon (1997, p. 388), an early proponent of WAC, cites Soven's *Write to Learn: A Guide to Writing Across the Curriculum* (1996) as "a concise guide to teaching writing in the disciplines and to developing a campuswide program."

Complementing writing centers, course offerings, and WAC are various publication resources such as the *ADE Bulletin* (published by the Association of Departments of English), the *CEA Forum* (published by the College English Association), and *WPA: Writing Program Administration,* which are written with the academic administrator in mind, not the field specialist. These sources keep deans and department chairs current on practical matters as well as the most recent trends in the field of composition.

Last and maybe most important to the future of composition studies is technology. Computers and information/instructional technology have already affected the teaching and learning of writing. The increasing use of e-mail, the Internet, and computer-aided writing by industry, education, and private citizens will have enormous influence on how writing is taught and how knowledge is retrieved and created.

With the explosion of information access available through the Internet and the increased dependence on graphical representation of information (as opposed to textual representation), how will the writing instructor in the twenty-first century teach audience awareness and purpose when texts will not necessarily be written to specific audiences, or effective arrangement when texts are no longer required to be read linearly (where every other word is linked to some other Web site)? Electronic communication technologies can make information access easily available, and immediate access to information from the office or the home has enormous implications for the teaching of writing.

Blurton (1994) offers methods for incorporating easy information access into the curriculum in his article. "Using the Internet for Teaching, Learning, and Research." The research paper, for example, gives students practice in information retrieval and deciding what information was pertinent to a given writing task. With the abundance of information to sift through, students must learn the most efficient ways to use the Internet.

Excellent sources exist, both institutional and on the World Wide Web, for learning about technology and writing. Organizations such as The Alliance for Computers and Writing (http://english.ttu.edu/acw/acw.html) and the American Association of Higher Education (http://www.aahe.org) provide discussion lists that individuals in higher education can use for a dialogue on the most recent development on computers, technology, pedagogy and writing. Nationally funded projects such as the Epiphany Project (http://mason.gmu.edu/~epiphany/) offer information and discussion on strategies and structures for pedagogical change in the age of electronic text.

## Implications and Potential Solutions

Some of the benefits of writing across the curriculum are that students learn in communal, active, and collaborative settings; faculty, through writing workshops, meet each other in "settings that neutralize traditional university hierarchies and cut across both disciplinary and college lines"; and institutions may achieve balance in their expectations of faculty, create language-centered curricula, and alter reward structures to value the time teachers spend on improving their teaching (Fulwiler, 1994, pp. 448–450).

With all of these benefits to students, faculty, and institutions, problems still face those teachers who wish to (or are required to) incorporate writing into their courses: growing class size, limited resources, lack of faculty development initiatives, and training, to name a few. Often, institutions try to bestow the benefits of writing by decreeing some official program (for example, writing across the curriculum, writing emphasis, and writing in the disciplines programs). Without some faculty development structure in place, faculty often feel they must add the job of English teacher to their own or just add writing to their courses (Thaiss, 1994, p. 476).

One way to alleviate these concerns is through faculty development. Thaiss suggests that "rather than doling out release time and reduced student loads to faculty who teach writing-intensive courses, spend the release time or some other suitable reward on faculty development workshops and on continuing coordination of the faculty development program" (p. 477). Effective training of faculty includes offering workshops and short seminars that present and model classroom writing activities, such as the one-minute paper, which is assigned at the end of a class and returned to students with feedback at the start of the next class (pp. 200–201). Technology can also be implemented. Students can collaborate and exchange documents by e-mail. Teachers can set up discussion lists in which class members post written responses to the rest of the class. These exercises are good examples of how writing enhances learning.

Another solution is reforming general education requirements to help make written communication a vital component of the core. Often, general education requirements force nonmajors to seek upper-division courses in order to fulfill a distribution requirement without sufficient background. Students become frustrated and faculty become dissatisfied with student performance. Portland State University offers a model for comprehensive reform in general education. Included in their statement of purpose for the general education program, they list "use various forms of communication for learning and expression" (White, 1994, p. 177) and meet that goal by having a writing requirement. Portland State's writing requirement "does not include a separate set of courses identified as writing courses" but, rather, works on "the premise that an essential component for all courses included in the program will be a demonstrable and substantial emphasis on communication as a component of learning" (p. 196). In other words, the writing requirement is built into all of the general education coursework.

Lastly, creating alliances within academic and nonacademic institutions will help create coherence between secondary education, higher education, and the business community. Wayne State's collaboration with local business and industry helped improve their professional writing program (Couture and others, 1985). Within the university itself, creating writing internships with various businesses and developing linked courses between different disciplines reveals to students the importance of writing in their learning process as well as for their life after graduation.

## Conclusion

As Faigley predicted in 1986, "If the process movement is to continue to influence the teaching of writing . . . , it must take a broader conception of writing, one that understands writing processes are historically dynamic—not psychic states, cognitive routines, or neutral social relationships" (p. 537). The last three sections of *Making Thinking Visible: Writing, Collaborative Planning, and Classroom Inquiry* (Flower, Wallace, Norris, and Burnett, 1994) serve as a response to Faigley's call. They provide insight for future direction on how to narrow the gap between academic writing and nonacademic writing, and in the process create coherence in the teaching of the discipline of writing—coherence in secondary-, postsecondary-, and real-world-level writing. These sections support the synthesis of the various theories of the composing process and the use of their related pedagogical practices.

The writing classroom is becoming more culturally diverse, the concern for the study of nonacademic writing continues to grow, the constraints that face effective writing instruction are numerous and varied, and the writing skills that college graduates need to succeed in the workplace and in society continue to be examined in different contexts (theoretical, practical, professional and business, and political). All of these present challenges and opportunities in the pursuit of educating students to write effectively.

## References

Anderson, P. V. "What Survey Research Tells Us About Writing at Work." In L. Odell and D. Goswami (eds.), *Writing in Nonacademic Settings*. New York: Guilford, 1985.

Anson, C. M., Schwiebert, J. E., and Williamson, M. M. *Writing Across the Curriculum: An Annotated Bibliography.* Westport, Conn.: Greenwood, 1993.

Barabas, C. *Technical Writing in a Corporate Culture: A Study of the Nature of Information.* Norwood, N.J.: Ablex, 1990.

Berthoff, A. *Forming, Thinking, Writing: The Composing Imagination.* Upper Montclair, N.J.: Boynton, 1982.

Bitzer, L. "The Rhetorical Situation." *Philosophy and Rhetoric,* 1968, *1,* 1–14.

Bizzell, P. and Herzberg, B. (eds.). *The Bedford Bibliography for Teachers of Writing.* (4th ed.) Boston: St. Martin's Press, 1996.

Bizzell, P., and Herzberg, B. (eds.). *The Bedford Bibliography for Teachers of Writing.* (3rd ed.) Boston: St. Martin's Press, 1991.

Blalock, G. (ed.). *The Bedford Handbook for Teachers of Writing.* (4th ed.) Boston: St. Martin's Press, 1994.

Blurton, C. "Using the Internet for Teaching, Learning, and Research." In D. F. Halpern and Associates, *Changing College Classrooms: New Teaching and Learning Strategies for the Increasingly Complex World.* San Francisco: Jossey-Bass, 1994.

Booth, W. "The Rhetorical Stance." *College Composition and Communication,* 1963, *14,* 139–145.

Brown, S. C., Selfe, C. L., and Selzer, J. "Interchange." *ATTW Bulletin,* 1994, *5* (1), 5–12.

Bruffee, K. "Collaborative Learning and the 'Conversation of Mankind.'" *College English,* 1984, *46* (7), 635–652.

Bruffee, K. "Social Construction, Language, and the Authority of Knowledge: A Bibliographic Essay." *College English,* 1986, *48* (8), 772–790.

Coles, W., Jr. "Freshman Composition: The Circle of Unbelief." *College English,* 1969, *31,* 134–142.

Connors, R. J., Ede, L. S., and Lunsford, A. A. (eds.). *Essays on Classical Rhetoric and Modern Discourse.* Carbondale: Southern Illinois University Press, 1984.

Cooper, M. M. "The Ecology of Writing." *College English,* 1986, *48,* 364–375.

Corbett, E. *Classical Rhetoric for the Modern Student.* (3rd ed.) New York: Oxford University Press, 1990.

Couture, B., Goldstein, J. R., Malone, E. L., Nelson, B., and Quiroz, S. "Building a Professional Writing Program Through a University-Industry Collaborative." In L. Odell and D. Goswami (eds.), *Writing in Nonacademic Settings.* New York: Guilford, 1985.

Crowley, S. *Ancient Rhetorics for Contemporary Students.* New York: Macmillan, 1994.

Daiker, D., Kerek, A., Morenberg, M., and Sommers, J. *The Writer's Options: Combining to Composing.* (5th ed.) New York: HarperCollins, 1994.

Dawkins, J. "Teaching Punctuation as a Rhetorical Tool." *College Composition and Communication,* 1995, *46,* 4, 533–548.

Ede, L., and Lunsford, A. "Audience Addressed/Audience Invoked: The Role of Audience in Composition Theory and Pedagogy." *College Composition and Communication,* 1984, *35,* 155–171.

Eden, R., and Mitchell, R. "Paraphrasing for the Reader." *College Composition and Communication,* 1986, *37,* 416–430, 441.

Elbow, P. *Writing Without Teachers.* New York: Oxford, 1973.

Elbow, P. "Closing My Eyes as I Speak: An Argument for Ignoring Audience." *College English,* 1987, *49,* 50–69.

Emig, J. *The Composing Processes of Twelfth Graders.* Urbana, Ill.: National Council of Teachers of English, 1971.

Faigley, L. "Competing Theories of Process: A Critique and a Proposal." *College English,* 1986, *48,* 527–542.

Faigley, L., Cherry, R. D., Jolliffe, D. A., and Skinner, A. M. *Assessing Writers' Knowledge and Processes of Composing.* Norwood, N.J.: Ablex Publishing, 1985.

Fleckenstein, K. S. "An Appetite for Coherence: Arousing and Fulfilling Desires." *College Composition and Communication,* 1992, *43,* 81–87.

Flower, L. *The Construction of Negotiated Meaning: A Social Cognitive Theory of Writing.* Carbondale: Southern Illinois University Press, 1994.

Flower, L., and Hayes, J. R. "The Dynamics of Composing: Making Plans and Juggling Constraints." In L. Gregg and E. Steinberg (eds.), *Cognitive Processes in Writing: An Interdisciplinary Approach.* Hillsdale, N.J.: Erlbaum, 1980.

Flower, L., and Hayes, J. R. "A Cognitive Process Theory of Writing." *College Composition and Communication,* 1981, *32,* 365–387.

Flower, L., Wallace, D. L., Norris, L., and Burnett, R. (eds.). *Making Thinking Visible: Writing, Collaborative Planning, and Classroom Inquiry.* Urbana, Ill.: National Council of Teachers of English, 1994.

Fulwiler, T. "The Quiet and Insistent Revolution: Writing Across the Curriculum." In G. Blalock, (ed.) *The Bedford Handbook for Teachers of Writing.* (4th ed.) Boston: St. Martin's Press, 1994.

Goodsell, A. S., Maher, M. R., Tinto, V., Smith, B. L., and MacGregor, J. (eds.). *Collaborative Learning: A Sourcebook for Higher Education.* State College: National Center on Postsecondary Teaching, Learning, and Assessment, The Pennsylvania State University, 1992.

Harris, M. "Talking in the Middle: Why Writers Need Writing Tutors." *College English,* 1995, *57,* 27–42.

Harris, M. *Teaching One-to-One: The Writing Conference.* Urbana, Ill.: National Council of Teachers of English, 1986.

Hawisher, G., and Selfe, C. L. (eds.). *CCCC Bibliography of Composition and Rhetoric, 1993.* Carbondale: Southern Illinois University Press, 1995.

Hillocks, G., Jr. *Research on Written Composition.* Urbana, Ill.: National Council of Teachers of English, 1986.

Hult, C., and Kinkead, J. (eds.). "Writing Centers Online." *Computers and Composition,* 1995, *12,* (2).

Jones, E., Hoffman, S., Melander-Moore, L., Ratcliff, G., Tibbetts, S., and Click, B.A.L., III. *Identifying College Graduates' Essential Skills in Writing, Speech and Listening, and Critical Thinking.* University Park: National Center on Postsecondary Teaching, Learning, and Assessment, The Pennsylvania State University, 1994.

Knoblauch, C. H., and Brannon, L. *Rhetorical Traditions and the Teaching of Writing.* Upper Montclair, N.J.: Boynton, 1984.

Kolln, M. *Rhetorical Grammar: Grammatical Choices, Rhetorical Effects.* New York: Macmillan, 1991.

Larson, R. L. "Selected Bibliography of Research and Writing About the Teaching of Composition." *College Composition and Communication,* 1988, *39* (3), 316–336.

Macrorie, K. *Writing to Be Read.* New York: Hayden, 1968.

Maimon, E. "Teaching 'Writing Across the Curriculum.'" In J. G. Gaff and J. L. Ratcliff and Associates (eds.), *The Handbook of the Undergraduate Curriculum: A Comprehensive Guide to Purposes, Structures, Practices, and Change.* San Francisco: Jossey-Bass, 1997.

McClelland, B. W., and Donovan, T. R. (eds.). *Perspectives on Research and Scholarship in Composition.* New York: Modern Language Association, 1985.

Moran, M. G., and Lundsford, R. E. (eds.). *Research in Composition and Rhetoric: A Bibliographic Sourcebook.* Westport, Conn.: Greenwood, 1984.

Mullin, J., and Wallace, R. (eds.). *Intersections: Theory-Practice in the Writing Center.* Urbana, Ill.: National Council of Teachers of English, 1994.

Murphy, C., and Law, J. (eds.). *Landmark Essays on Writing Centers.* Davis, Calif.: Hermagoras Press, 1995.

Murray, D. M. "Write Before Writing." *College Composition and Communication,* 1978, *29,* 375–382.

Odell, L., and Goswami, D. (eds.). *Writing in Nonacademic Settings.* New York: Guilford, 1985.

Olson, G. A. (ed.). *Writing Centers: Theory and Administration.* Urbana, Ill.: National Council of Teachers of English, 1989.

Ong, W. "The Writer's Audience Is Always a Fiction." *PMLA,* 1975, *90,* 9–21.

Penrose, A. M., and Sitko, B. M. (eds.). *Hearing Ourselves Think: Cognitive Research in the College Writing Classroom.* New York: Oxford University Press, 1993.

Perl, S. (ed.). *Landmark Essays on the Writing Process.* Davis, Calif.: Hermagoras Press, 1994.

Rose, M. (ed.) *When a Writer Can't Write: Studies in Writer's Block and Other Composing Process Problems.* New York: Guilford Press, 1985.

Sommers, N. "Revision Strategies of Student Writers and Experienced Adult Writers." *College Composition and Communication,* 1980, *31,* 378–388.

Soven, M. *Write to Learn: A Guide to Writing Across the Curriculum.* Albany, N.Y.: South-Western College Publishing, 1996.

Steward, D. "Prose with Integrity: A Primary Objective." *College Composition and Communication,* 1969, *20,* 223–227.

Tate, G. (ed.). *Teaching Composition: Twelve Bibliographic Essays.* Fort Worth: Texas Christian University Press, 1987.

Thaiss, C. "The Future of Writing Across the Curriculum." In G. Blalock (ed.), *The Bedford Handbook for Teachers of Writing.* (4th ed.) Boston: St. Martin's Press, 1994.

Tobin, L., and Newkirk, T. (eds.). *Taking Stock: The Writing Process Movement in the 90s.* Portsmouth, N.H.: Heinemann, 1994.

White, C. R. "A Model for Comprehensive Reform in General Education: Portland State University." *Journal of General Education,* 1994, *43* (3), 168–229.

Williams, J. *Style: Ten Lessons in Clarity and Grace.* (4th ed.) New York: HarperCollins, 1995.

BENJAMIN A. L. CLICK III *is assistant professor of English and writing center coordinator at the University of Wisconsin–La Crosse.*

*National educational outcomes research on reading competence has*
*implications for policy, curriculum design, and teaching and learning*
*assessment.*

# Raising Expectations for Critical Reading

*JoAnn Carter-Wells*

College reading has had a very long history, with its roots in a program developed at Wellesley College in 1894. Even though there is a wide body of instruction-centered research and practice, college reading is often misunderstood on college campuses. However, in the past five to ten years, there has been growing national recognition of this field as truly developmental (not remedial) and credible in terms of curriculum, research, and institutional stature (Maya, 1995; Wyatt, 1992). The emergence of the freshman year curriculum at many institutions and general education revisions focusing on essential communication skills of students represent some of the components of this resurgence.

A better understanding of the role of reading as a college outcome is arising because of workplace expectations and many leading professional accreditation agencies, such as the Accreditation Board for Engineering and Technology (Engineering Accreditation Commission, 1996) and the Accounting Education Change Commission (Gainen and Locatelli, 1995). Additional external forces include the U.S. Department of Labor's SCANS report (1991) and various other reports related to requisite workplace communication skills. These reports all reaffirm the importance of communication skills (including reading) as the foundation skills and workplace competencies that employers value. Employers want people in their organizations who "read and understand literal and implied meanings of textual material similar to that found in the workplace" (Nowlin, 1996, p. 5). The recent emergence of information competence expectations may also support the viability of college reading as an outcome and the credibility of related curricula (Batson and Bass, 1996; Curzon, 1995). The most important work for raising expectations for critical reading outcomes, however, is that recently funded by the National Center on Education Statistics (NCES) and conducted by the National Center on Postsecondary Teaching, Learning, and Assessment (Jones, Dougherty, and Fantaske, 1997).

Recent research and expanded conceptual frameworks and models are beginning to clarify necessary reading outcomes (Carter-Wells, 1989; Lewis and Carter-Wells, 1987; Carter-Wells, 1992; Maxwell, 1995/6; Mulcahy-Ernt, 1990; O'Hear, 1993; Pugh and Pawan, 1991; Rubin, 1991). These models have been characterized as *bottom-up* (breaking the written code), *top-down* (using the reader's prior knowledge and linguistic competence), or *interactive* (both occurring simultaneously). *Metacognition,* or the reader's awareness of the process of reading and learning, is another important theoretical component today (Mulcahy-Ernt, 1990).

One of the models that relates to the college level is a developmental conceptualization model of the reading process known as Stage 5—Construction and Reconstruction—for ages eighteen and above.

Stage 5 can be seen as reading that is essentially constructive. From reading what others say, the readers construct knowledge for themselves. The processes depend on analysis, synthesis, and judgment (Chall, 1983, p. 23).

That is, reading is used for one's own needs and for both professional and personal purposes. Reading serves to integrate one's knowledge with that of others, to synthesize it, and to create new knowledge. Chall's conceptualization of the stages of reading development begins at the preschool level (Stage 0—Prereading) and advances through K–12. It includes Stage 3—Reading for Learning, for grades 4 through 8, and Stage 4—Multiple Viewpoints, at the high school level.

Many of these models also incorporate the historical perspective of reading as a reasoning and problem-solving process incorporating inference, interpretation, concept formation, conceptual ability, evaluation, and metacognition (Lewis, 1991; Paul, 1992). They also assume developmental and intellectual maturation of college students, as originally presented by William Perry (1970). There is a growing recognition of reading and writing as *modes of reasoning* that facilitate learning.

## Results of the National Reading Goals Research

A review of the research using the Reading Goals Inventory (Jones, 1996) is presented in this section with specific observations and conclusions. To further corroborate the relationships between critical reading and critical thinking, items categorized as Interpretation, Analysis, Evaluation, Inference, Reflection, and Dispositions, which were also identified as important in the critical thinking outcomes study and presented on pages 129–153 of that document (Jones and others, 1994), are coded as CT.

**Reading Materials.** These materials are described as specific "media used for communicating information" (Jones, 1996, p. 1) that students should be able to understand and evaluate with a minimum amount of training. All the groups agreed as to the importance of being able to read such diverse materials as memos, instruction manuals, journal articles, computer media (World Wide Web), technical reports, advertisements, and graphic designs (for example, blueprints and maps). The controversial areas of disagreement between faculty and policymakers were data on graphs and charts, with policymakers indicating that these were more important than did the faculty. It is important to note the recognition of the importance of computers as a communication tool for college students.

**Reading for Content.** The inventory defines this category as "understanding printed documents or other material" (Jones, 1996, p. 1). There was general agreement that college students should be able to understand the topic of sentences or paragraphs, to make notes as they read, to vary their reading rates, and to display their understanding of a text in graphical forms such as maps and flowcharts. This seems inconsistent with the findings in the Reading Material section of the survey, in which there was disagreement as to the importance of using data in charts and graphs (Jones, 1996).

This was the section of the survey that yielded the greatest amount of disagreement between employers and faculty. Faculty felt more strongly about the importance of persisting while reading (a disposition as well), of recognizing relationships between concepts and terms or phrases, and of using background knowledge while reading texts. Also controversial were the skills of identifying the author's stated points of view and recognizing confusing language or devices such as metaphor, irony, and humor. Finally, the ability to create meaning through the use of imagination was more important for faculty.

**Interpretation.** *Interpretation* is focused on "understanding the meaning and significance of texts" (Jones, 1996, p. 2). All groups of participants felt that for effective interpretation, college graduates should be able to recognize contradictions or inconsistencies in a text (CT), to identify leading questions that are biased toward eliciting a preferred response (CT), and to use examples from prior experience to explain or remove ambiguities (CT). Once again, employers and faculty were unclear about the importance of four additional skills. Faculty felt more strongly than the employers that college students should be able to note similarities and differences between concepts and ideas, to organize information in categories or frameworks to facilitate understanding, and to identify emotional language and tone while reading.

**Analysis.** The Reading Goals Inventory states that *analysis* is "identifying the explicit and implied features in a reading, especially arguments or positions that put forth a conclusion" (Jones, 1996, p. 3). The survey participants agreed that the ability to identify the conclusions of an argument or position (CT) and the ability to decide whether a text provides support for a conclusion or opinion (CT) were essential reading outcomes. Again, employers and faculty had different perspectives on the importance of other analysis skills, including identifying both the author's interests, attitudes, and ideas and the stated or implied purposes of a text; identifying the reasons that support a conclusion; and analyzing the author's arguments or position to confirm or disconfirm their reasoning or results. Faculty tended to consider these to be more important than did employers.

**Evaluation.** *Evaluation* is the ability to judge and assess the credibility of a text and the strength of claims or positions (Jones, 1996, p. 4). There were many skills in this section of the inventory that all participants agreed upon. All participants felt that college students should be able to determine the assumption in an argument (CT) and evaluate the credibility of sources of information (CT). Other important skills are the ability to judge evidence (CT), the reasonableness and practicality of the author's position (CT), and the author's ability to anticipate possible objections and offer alternative explanations (CT).

**Inference.** *Inference* is the ability "to reason from what we know to form new knowledge, draw conclusions, solve problems, explain, decide and/or predict" (Jones, 1996, p.4). All participants felt that inference skills were important college reading outcomes. They agreed that college graduates should be able to formulate an opinion while considering divergent points of view (CT), use other resources as evidence to confirm or disconfirm an author's conclusion (CT), and identify cause-effect relationships (CT). Equally important are the skills of developing and using reliable, sound criteria for making judgments about a text (CT) and determining if there is sufficient evidence to form a conclusion (CT). However, there were disagreements among all groups as to the relative importance of identifying various components of a text, such as the details and the structure of information, and locating information to evaluate divergent opinions presented in the same text. Faculty and policymakers rated these more highly than employers did.

**Reflection.** *Reflection* is the metacognitive component of the survey that focuses on the ability to monitor one's comprehension and correct one's process of thinking (Jones, 1996, p. 5). The only skill that all participants felt to be essential for college students is the ability to identify their own strategies and opinions for understanding a text (CT). There was disagreement about all the other reflection skills on the survey, particularly between faculty and employers. Faculty participants seemed to be more aware of the importance of reflection while reading, which is a relatively new area of research and practice in the field.

**Dispositions.** *Dispositions* is the last category on the Reading Goals Inventory; it focuses on those "attitudes and inclinations that concern how college graduates use their reading skills" (Jones, 1996, p. 6). All groups seemed to have a better understanding of the role of dispositions than that of reflection in the reading process. There was agreement that college students should remain analytical when reading (CT), be willing to read for both personal and professional growth, strive to understand and consider divergent points of view (CT), include insights about other cultures when reading (CT), remain impartial when reading other points of view (CT), and select a suitable environment for their reading. Interestingly, faculty and employers disagreed about the importance of a college student's emotional response, empathy, perseverance, and inquisitive demeanor while reading. Finally, although there are not direct language items in the critical thinking outcomes survey, there are items that have linkages to these reading dispositions. In particular are the abilities to be open-minded, to strive to understand and consider divergent points of view, to be fair-minded, and to be curious and inquisitive as to how and why things work.

**Observations.** There are obvious observations from a review of these results. Employers are not generally aware of the complexity of reading as a process or of the roles and importance of reflection and dispositions when reading. They seem to value more the product than the process, as is also presented in the writing outcomes research (Jones and others, 1994). This work also helps to confirm and corroborate the construct of critical reading as critical thinking and many of the current theories of the reading process. The emphasis on study reading in many college reading classes may be too narrowly presented for adequate workplace linkages. Also, conflicting information is emerging as to the importance of the linkages between new computer technology and requisite reading skills as information competencies. Both the specific language and overlap in importance of many of the identified skills reflect the recursive nature of reading as a process and not just specific, isolated skills. Finally, there is additional confirmation of college reading as both a complex process that requires further study and as a viable and credible college student communications skill outcome and competency.

## Implications

There are enormous implications from this landmark research for institutional and professional policy, curriculum design, teaching and learning, assessment, and future research. Obviously, dissemination is also essential. Professional associations and institutions of higher education could even consider utilizing this work in future national conferences or funded research programs to expand the dialogue on reading as a viable and essential college student outcome and competency.

**Institutional and Professional Policy.** College reading and learning as a profession has often been viewed as being on the periphery of the academy, and its programs are usually housed in a nonacademic unit on a campus. The power of including reading as a communication skill in National Education Goal 6.5 is that reading is finally recognized as an "outcome" competency equal to the more traditional areas such as writing, speaking, and listening. It is no longer just an entry, basic, or developmental (often interpreted as "remedial") skill. Reading and learning professionals should seize this moment and be willing to provide leadership on their campuses in new ways to respond to the exciting challenges and issues of this era. In many ways, this profession is finally coming of age, as outlined by Arthur Cohen in his keynote address in to the Western College Reading and Learning Association (1987). College reading professionals are uniquely trained in teaching, learning, and assessment. Their training is grounded in both formal certification and research as well as informal classroom application and practice over many decades. They are the true practitioners of postsecondary learning throughout this century. As learning is becoming "preeminent" in the language of the academy today, this profession has a long history to support its claims to expertise.

The themes of this new involvement should be *awareness, language,* and *linkage.* There are many misassumptions about the reading process, and communication of this outcomes research to the higher education community and its stakeholders provides the opportunity to create a new awareness of reading as a viable competency expectation. However, this awareness needs to be informed with new language. As reading and learning professionals have observed over the years, there are major connotative problems with the term *developmental.* Some terminology emanating from the new paradigms of information competency, critical literacy, and lifelong learning provide groundwork for expanded and more contemporary reconceptualizations of college reading. The current trend of revised standards in the profession can provide the venue for consideration of relevant language issues. However, campus awareness with contemporary language can only be nurtured and developed through critical linkages that are both theoretical and practical. College reading professionals often have had to operate in isolation on many campuses. This research provides another opportunity for change. There have always been theoretical or integrative/interdisciplinary linkages with the fields of psychology—adult development and cognitive psychology—and with rhetoric. The emergence of critical thinking and lifelong learning in the curriculum is another obvious linkage. But this NCES work provides additional groundwork for more integrated campus linkages that will better inform curricular, and resulting structural, changes. Obvious practical linkages include development of workplace programs beyond literacy needs; K–16 connections and partnerships particularly focused on academic preparation curricula; and student-employer partnerships in programs such as service learning, internships, and cooperative education.

**Curriculum Design.** This research, linked with the movements toward revision of general education programs, provides the opportunity for innovative curriculum development and integration that is both horizontal and vertical across the curriculum. College reading is an obvious inclusion in thematic general education clusters; in freshman orientation/transition/bridge as well as senior-year classes; in intern, service learning, and team project seminars; and in cornerstone (major) or capstone (senior) courses. Examples of early innovative projects are the Coppin Critical Reading Project at Coppin State College (Kelley, 1989) and the Critical Literacy Project at Oakton Community College (Storinger and Boehm, 1988). Both of these projects focused on developmental activities designed to help faculty reevaluate their teaching strategies and redesign courses in general education to include critical reading, writing, and thinking. Academic courses in reading and learning for college credit can be developed under the language, communication skills, or critical thinking requirements of general education (as they have often been done in California). Because of this linkage with the workplace and lifelong learning, the notion of designing sophisticated college reading and learning curricula for transfer is easily satisfied. Finally, institutions revising their general education programs can use the individual Reading Goals Inventory with groups of faculty to help guide decisions on specific competencies or goals in their programs.

**Teaching and Learning.** Although college reading professionals are well-grounded in good teaching and learning practices, additional observations from the research are important to reinforce. The inclusion of active learning focusing on the process and dispositions of reading and learning are imperative. Activities that require students to reflect on the communication needs of their majors, careers, or professions can enhance lifelong learning along with increased use of computer technology for information gathering, processing, and communicating and teamwork or group project application. Other examples include ongoing informal self-assessment and evaluation of one's reading and learning in classes, such as that presented in the Classroom Assessment literature (Angelo and Cross, 1993). Presentations and discussions of National Education Goal 6.5 and the results of the reading outcomes research to students at all academic levels add credibility and viability to those class requirements and activities that focus on the process of students' reading and learning instead of just on a product or outcome, such as that usually required on an objective test or essay.

These research results should also add credibility to both the role and the importance of essential communication and critical thinking skills throughout the curriculum. Finally, reading professionals can adapt this research for use in their classrooms when designing their own materials, as is popular with custom publishing today. They can also collaborate more effectively with publishers to develop materials that correspond to this goal and the outcomes research.

**Assessment.** Finally, the reconceptualization of college reading as an outcome could provide the forum for renewed interest in developing better college reading assessment measures that could more adequately tap both disciplinary needs and general workplace expectations. These results can be used in the development of both formal and informal measures, including self-assessment indicators.

In addition, critical thinking assessment is a relatively new field of research and design. It seems appropriate, then, that the knowledge and expertise gained from the development of reading instruments (primarily K–12) throughout this century can be applied to the development of better critical thinking instruments. There are many concerns with the current critical thinking instruments. One important concern is that they have a high correlation with reading and that many of the prompts and items are very similar in design to college reading instruments, such as the Nelson-Denny Reading Test. We need to be careful of the interpretations of those instruments. Are we tapping reading or thinking? Better measures are needed to integrate the current theoretical perspective of postsecondary reading as an outcome expectation with the renewed emphasis on critical thinking as mandated by National Education Goal 6.5. Current instruments still emphasize individual and discrete skills and do not truly reflect reading as a process or the dispositions of reading.

The current language of *communication,* or *information processing,* is a very powerful way to reconceptualize *reading* so that it will have more credibility in the assessment field as well as with the public at large. How we define *reading* and, more importantly, *critical reading* is a very important underpinning of the assessment problem today (Lewis, 1991). Reading is routinely labeled as an entry skill in placement tests or as a foundational skill but not as an outcome competency or expectation for success in the workplace. The true developmental nature of reading is not recognized in the same way that the developmental nature of writing has been. Many of the commercially developed assessment instruments for general education include sections commonly labeled *reasoning and communication skills.* To effectively complete some of the comprehensive as well as authentic subtests and measures, students need to be able to interpret, analyze, and evaluate *written* information before responding and applying the information in some observational performance—that is, they need to be able to *read* at high levels of proficiency. Assessment instruments rarely identify *reading* as a skill at the college level; rather, it becomes *communicating.* If reading and writing are modes of reasoning, then reasoning from written information requires a high level of competency and processing print. It is difficult to separate and observe specific and discrete skills required in communicating, and they are usually recursive processes. It is obvious that the results of this landmark research coupled with the specific items on the Reading Goals Inventory (Jones, 1996) provide a wonderful opportunity for the assessment community to create a forum for conversation with the workforce. Together they could develop more credible general education outcomes and reading competency criteria and assessment tools with both academic- and workplace-specific applications and examples.

A specific classroom application of this work is the use of the Reading Goals Inventory for self-assessment and teaching and learning. Students can review the specific reading competencies and consider their application and use in either their academic or workplace environments.

**Future Research.** It is obvious that these NCES outcomes results help clarify future directions and many avenues for researchers in college reading and learning. For example, what specific reading skills are necessary to effectively utilize the World Wide Web and the Internet? What are the reading competencies required by specific professional disciplines such as nursing, engineering, and accounting as generally specified by their accreditation agencies? What are the behaviors that are common to critical thinking and all the communication skills, including reading? What does it mean to assess, evaluate, judge, or interpret in each of these areas and what do they have in common? What might be the components of a theoretical construct linking critical thinking and reading, writing, and speaking? What are their common underpinnings, such as organizing information or seeing relationships? Finally, what are the adult developmental theories that correlate or better explain the critical reading process as a constructionist, or meaning-making, and lifelong learning process?

Finally, it is impossible to overemphasize the value of this landmark work to the college reading and learning profession as a whole. Nor is it wise to ignore the power, potential, and timing of this research for moving college reading into the national outcomes/competency dialogue amid this unprecedented emphasis in postsecondary education on student learning and standards.

## References

Angelo, T. A., and Cross, K. P. *Classroom Assessment Techniques: A Handbook for College Teachers.* (2nd ed.) San Francisco: Jossey-Bass, 1993.

Batson, T., and Bass, R. "Teaching and Learning in the Computer Age." *Change,* Mar./Apr. 1996, pp. 42–47.

Carter-Wells, J. "Academic Preparation for College: What We Know and Where We Need to Go." *Review of Research in Developmental Education,* 1989, 7 (2), 3–6.

Carter-Wells, J. "A Critique of 'No Guru, No Method, No Teacher': The Communication Domain and the NACSL." Paper presented at the National Center for Education Statistics Workshop on the Assessment of Higher Order Thinking and Communication Skills of College Graduates: Preliminary Listing of Skills and Levels of Proficiency, Washington, D.C., Nov. 17, 1992.

Chall, J. *Stages of Reading Development.* New York: McGraw-Hill, 1983.

Cohen, A. M. "Twenty Years of Progress Toward a Discipline: WCRLA Keynote Address." *Journal of College Reading and Learning,* 1987, *20,* 1–7.

Curzon, S. *Information Competence in the CSU: A Report.* Long Beach: Chancellor's Office, California State University, 1995.

Engineering Accreditation Commission. *Engineering Criteria 2000.* Baltimore, Md.: Engineering Accreditation Commission, 1996.

Gainen, J., and Locatelli, P. *Assessment for the New Curriculum: A Guide for Professional Accounting Programs.* Accounting Education Series, Vol. 11. Sarasota, Fla.: Accounting Education Change Commission and American Accounting Association, 1994.

Jones, E. A. *Reading Goals Inventory.* University Park: National Center on Postsecondary Teaching, Learning, and Assessment, The Pennsylvania State University, 1996.

Jones, E. A., Dougherty, C., and Fantaske, P. *Defining Essential Critical Reading and Problem-Solving Outcomes: Perspectives of Faculty, Employers, and Policymakers.* University Park: National Center on Postsecondary Teaching, Learning, and Assessment, The Pennsylvania State University, 1997.

Jones, E. A., Hoffman, S., Melander-Moore, L., Ratcliff, G., Tibbetts, S., and Click, B.A.L. *Identifying College Graduates' Essential Skills in Writing, Speech and Listening and Critical Thinking: Final Project Report.* University Park: National Center on Postsecondary Teaching, Learning, and Assessment, The Pennsylvania State University, 1994.

Kelley, D. G. "Coppin Critical Reading Project of Coppin State College." Project Report. Wasington, D.C.: American Association of State Colleges and Universities, 1989 (ED 306 852)

Lewis, J. "Redefining Critical Reading for College Critical Thinking Courses." *Journal of Reading,* 1991, *34* (6), 420–423.

Lewis, J., and Carter-Wells, J. "A Causal Model of Reading Achievement and Expository Writing Performance Among Selected College Freshmen." *Journal of College Reading and Learning,* 1987, *20,* 36–46.

Maxwell, M. "New Insights About Teaching College Reading: A Review of Recent Research." *Journal of College Reading and Learning,* 1995/96, 27 (1), 34–42.

Maya, A. Y. "Bridging the Academic Gap: An Historical Perspective of College Reading." Unpublished manuscript, Claremont Graduate School, 1995.

Mulcahy-Ernt, P. "What's New in Reading Research." *Journal of College Reading and Learning,* 1990, 22 (2), 37–48.

Nowlin, W. A. "Foundation Skills and Workplace Competence for the High-Tech Workplace." Paper presented at the 82nd Annual Conference of the Association of American Colleges and Universities, Washington, D.C., Jan. 11, 1996.

O'Hear, M. "College Reading Programs: The Past 25 Years." *Journal of College Reading and Learning,* 1993, 25 (2), 17–24.

Paul, R. W. *Critical Thinking: What Every Person Needs to Survive in a Rapidly Changing World.* (2nd ed.) Rohnert Park, Calif.: Center for Critical Thinking and Moral Critique, 1992.

Perry, W. G. *Forms of Intellectual and Ethical Development in the College Years.* Troy, Mo.: Holt, Rinehart and Winston, 1970.

Pugh, S. L., and Pawan, F. "Reading, Writing, and Academic Literacy." In R. F. Flippo and D. Caverly (eds.), *College Reading and Study Strategy Programs.* Newark, Del.: International Reading Association, 1991.

Rubin, M. "A Glossary of Education Terms Compiled by the CRLA Task Force on Professional Language for College Reading and Learning." *Journal of College Reading and Learning,* 1991, 23 (2), 1–13.

Storinger, R., and Boehm, L. "Critical Literacy Project: Final Report." Des Plaines, Ill.: Oakton Community College, 1988. (ED 317 243)

U.S. Department of Labor. 1991. *The Secretary's Commission on Achieving Necessary Skills: What Work Requires of Schools.* Washington, D.C.

Wyatt, M. "The Past, Present, and Future Need for College Reading Courses in the U.S." *Journal of Reading,* 1992, 36 (1), 10–19.

*JoANN CARTER-WELLS is professor of reading and coordinator of the undergraduate reading program at California State University, Fullerton, and past editor of the* Journal of College Reading and Learning.

*Complex problem solving often requires undergraduates to identify,*
*select, and implement alternatives.*

# Defining Expectations for Problem-Solving Skills

*B. Christopher Dougherty, Patti Fantaske*

Studies in cognitive psychology conducted in the 1960s and 1970s provided the impetus for researchers who attempted to codify the procedures, behaviors, and group dynamics associated with effective problem solving. In this chapter, we indicate how research over the past twenty years has shaped an understanding of effective problem-solving skills and their place in the undergraduate curriculum. We highlight selected authors who have informed a sense of effective problem-solving and its relationship to a variety of academic domains.

First, we provide an overview of the components of the problem-solving process, emphasizing that problem solving constitutes an iterative as opposed to a linear process. Second, we describe how individual characteristics influence the choices and outcomes associated with problem solving. Third, we discuss how an understanding of problem solving informs some innovative methods for teaching in college classrooms. We present the work of faculty who share their own innovative teaching techniques. Finally, we describe the role of problem solving in undergraduate education by focusing not only on math, science, and engineering (fields traditionally associated with the teaching of problem solving), but also on a variety of other disciplines that, among other things, require their students to effectively solve complex, poorly defined problems.

## Framework for Understanding Problem Solving

Along with the proliferation of definitions, frameworks, and step-by-step outlines of problem solving, there is considerable consensus regarding some of the

NEW DIRECTIONS FOR HIGHER EDUCATION, no. 96, Winter 1996 © Jossey-Bass Publishers important skills associated with effective problem solving. For example, it seems that all effective problem solving includes the search for a clear and concise statement of the problem along with the efficient generation, selection, and implementation of alternatives. We first explore what constitutes a problem.

A problem exists when an individual must complete a task but does not possess sufficient knowledge or experience to reach an appropriate solution. Problem solving occurs by means of mental processes such as acquiring information or defining procedures to arrive at an acceptable solution (Simon, 1978; Raaheim, 1974). The use of an analytical, step-by-step approach and clearly presented knowledge characterize a *well-structured* problem (Frederiksen, 1984; Simon, 1978). *Ill-structured* problems, in contrast, require the use of a combination of intuition, experience, and expertise to determine that a problem exists. Ill-structured problems also require the acquisition of knowledge and identification of the procedures needed to generate alternatives and choose a solution (Frederiksen, 1984; Simon, 1978). These problems (often referred to as "real world" or "fuzzy" problems) present a challenge for even the most expert problem solvers (Sternberg and Horvath, 1995).

In the leading cognitive psychology research targeted at identifying the components of the problem-solving process, researchers studied the behaviors of problem solvers through the use of "think aloud" protocols in which the solvers verbalized the steps taken while attempting to find solutions to various problems. The framework used for our discussion of problem solving is derived from the definitions of the process provided by these authors (for example, Newell and Simon, 1972; Simon, 1978; Frederiksen, 1984). We present a framework that highlights the abilities college students should possess to identify, choose, and implement solutions. This framework does not imply that problem solving progresses in steps executed one after the other. Instead, effective problem solvers will revisit and refine their definition of a problem and possible solutions as they move through the process (Hayes, 1989). We turn first to a discussion of the initial components in a successful problem-solving process: understanding the problem.

**Understanding the Problem.**  Problem solving is frequently initiated by the recognition that a problem exists. At some point, problem solvers must define the problem, search their memories for previous experiences solving similar problems, and understand the goals associated with solving the problem (Whimbey and Lochhead, 1991). Simon (1978) suggests that individuals create a problem space, or a representation of the components of a problem, in order to work on possible solutions. This representation will lead them to recall situations from memory that relate specifically to the problem as they understand it. In the case of well-structured problems, instructions help determine the problem space.

**Background Knowledge and Information Needed.**  In addition to searching memory and understanding goals for a specific problem, an individual must begin to gather the information needed to arrive at a well-considered solution. Success in gathering background knowledge depends, in part, on how effectively the solver represents the critical features of the task in the problem space. By effectively limiting the problem space, the individual constrains his or her behavior by defining acceptable strategies, setting goals, and managing the proliferation of alternatives for solution (Simon, 1978).

The knowledge needed to solve different types of problems varies considerably. Some problems require domain-specific knowledge in which information about the subject matter of the problem becomes necessary. Hegarty (1991), for example, differentiates conceptual knowledge and procedural knowledge as two types of domain-specific knowledge needed to solve problems. *Conceptual knowledge* includes knowledge of the theories and principles associated with a given domain. *Procedural knowledge,* on the other hand, represents the capacity to execute problem-solving operations. Other problems may require *tacit knowledge,* or practical know-how acquired through informal learning, personal experience, or the guidance of a mentor or colleague (Wagner, 1991). When using tacit knowledge to solve real-world problems, experience often indicates whether the solver can readily accomplish a particular task and will similarly dictate the amount of effort required to complete that task (Lesgold and Lajoie, 1991).

Complex problem solving often requires the development of both structural knowledge and strategic knowledge (Funke, 1991). Structural knowledge describes the functional or causal relationships between variables and usually comes as the result of hypothesis-formation and hypothesis-evaluation processes. Strategic knowledge addresses the solver's concern with applying information and developing a course of action for solving a problem that depends on previous experiences. Bloom and Broder (1950) found that the greatest gains in problem-solving performance derived from increased information, which suggests that a lack of information, or structural knowledge, constitutes the major problem-solving barrier easiest to identify and overcome in the case of many developing problem solvers.

**Generating Possible Solutions.** Problem solving requires the integrated use of thinking skills and an appropriate knowledge base (Rubinstein and Firstenberg, 1987). Outstanding thinking skills can produce novel solutions from limited information, whereas poor thinking skills may fail to produce solutions, even with an abundance of information (Newmann, 1991). Although the problem space constrains problem-solving efforts, the generation of solutions often calls for creativity and a willingness to avoid convention (Goldenberg, 1993; Kaufmann, 1979; Raaheim, 1974). The solver must learn to balance these efforts with the preservation of a sense of direction (Goldenberg, 1993), keeping in mind that more than one acceptable approach often exists. Experimentation and innovation often characterize the effective generation of alternative solutions (Harrison and Bramson, 1982).

**Choosing a Solution.** Before choosing a solution from multiple alternatives, individuals should identify factors that limit their behavior and use these constraints to evaluate possible solutions (Zacharakis-Jutz, 1983; Newmann, 1991). In order to do so, they must question the credibility of the premises upon which their solutions rest (Frederiksen, 1984; Newmann, 1991) and use evaluative criteria based on a wide range of expertise (Kay, 1994).

In choosing a solution, the solver should use criteria not only to evaluate, but also to rank possible solutions based on the probability and desirability of expected outcomes (Voss, 1991). They should form a reasoned plan for testing hypotheses (Frederiksen, 1984; Simon, 1978), then reduce the range of alternatives from which to choose (Voss, 1991; Newell and Simon, 1972). Finally, the solver should combine the factors identified by their analysis to produce a detailed solution (Zacharakis-Jutz, 1983).

**Evaluation of Solution and Making Recommendations.** Effective problem solvers should determine a means for evaluating alternatives to ensure the achievement of specified goals. This evaluation may include a review of the process that leads to further refinement and, eventually, a recommendation of an appropriate course of action (Zacharakis-Jutz, 1983). Although the scope of an undergraduate education may preclude the implementation of solutions, Norton, Bozeman, and Nadler (1980) suggest that any solution should include the seeds of its own continuing change and improvement. Therefore, when implemented, one should consider solutions provisional and subject to revision as indicated by changes in environmental factors.

The persons responsible for implementing solutions will bring their own style, habits, and skills to the process. Therefore, we briefly review additional research on problem solving that indicates how individual characteristics affect not only problem-solving performance but also the approaches and priorities that a variety of individuals bring to problem solving.

## Individual Influences on Problem Solving

Problem solving is a highly individualized process in which preferences and tendencies affect not only the ability to solve problems, but also the choice of an approach to problem solving. In Chapter Six, Peter A. Facione, Noreen C. Facione, and Carol Ann F. Giancarlo discuss the importance of various individual dispositions in determining the success of students in various learning tasks. In accordance with their findings, we wish to emphasize that patience, persistence, stress management, and a willingness to think creatively all affect the success of individual problem-solving efforts (Raaheim, 1974; Newmann, 1991; Swartz and Perkins, 1990).

In addition to personal characteristics that influence effective management of the problem-solving process, habits and preferences often determine how individuals and groups approach problem-solving tasks. Hoover and Feldhusen (1994) call the behavior associated with dispositions *cognitive style,* which includes individual characteristics such as tolerance for ambiguity, impulsiveness, and interest or motivation related to problem solving. Kirton (1989) defines two types of cognitive styles—*adaptors* and *innovators*—that refer to a person's preferred style of thinking as manifested during periods of change. Cognitive style, in this sense, is a preferred method of addressing problem solving. Individuals often will use adaptive behaviors when placed in a group whose members have cognitive styles different from their own. Alternatively, individuals will likely exhibit greater innovation in problem solving when placed in an environment that encourages creativity and divergent thinking.

In addition to the role that cognitive style plays in effective problem solving, creativity also facilitates the successful generation and implementation of complex solutions. Runco (1994) describes the relationship between problem solving and creativity, explaining that problem finding and problem solving relate to most creative efforts. The teaching of creativity often finds its way into problem solving in many undergraduate disciplines. For example, VanGundy (1987) emphasizes the importance of creative problem solving in the ill-defined domains of business, which require the individual to become familiar with all components of a problem to arrive at a successful solution. Creativity also seems to operate independently of constructs such as intelligence (Hayes, 1989). Therefore, instructors who focus on problem solving should encourage not only the effective processing of information but also the creative generation of ideas throughout the problem-solving process.

## Strategies for Teaching Problem Solving

Evidence from research suggests that educators can help students to refine their approach to problem solving in a number of ways. Most importantly, teachers should model their own problem-solving efforts and behaviors to their classes (Greenfield, 1987). In order to encourage students to think critically about their problem solving, instructors should also encourage discussion in the classroom as they work through problems (Costa and Lowery, 1989). In this case, professors should place students in a decision-making role, working together to move through each phase of the problem-solving process.

When solving ill-structured problems, the creative generation of a number of alternatives may present a significant challenge (Swartz and Perkins, 1990). In many cases, classroom participation facilitates the process of generating multiple solutions. Instructors should provide constructive feedback to students as they work together on solving problems, and they should also refer to previous problem-solving efforts to encourage students to search their memories for informative experiences (Zacharakis-Jutz, 1983). Professors may want to encourage students to work in pairs, with one partner verbalizing problem-solving procedures while the second monitors the other's thinking and provides feedback whenever appropriate (Whimbey and Lochhead, 1991).

Of course, effective problem solving depends not only on the modeling of problem-solving strategies, but also on the mastery of situations associated with various domains. Students who learn effective approaches to problem solving can subsequently apply their learning to a variety of situations (Hayes, 1980). As much as possible, instructors should encourage students to acquire and evaluate information to facilitate their problem solving, rather than simply providing students with information and procedures via traditional lecture methods (Newmann, 1991). As professors challenge their students to search for information through individual efforts rather than by taking notes, students become more likely to realize the importance of effective and efficient information gathering and its impact on problem solving in ill-structured domains.

Problem-solving strategies have become evident in some of the disciplines traditionally associated with undergraduate education. The teaching of effective problem solving belongs in a variety of academic domains, and the framework for problem solving mentioned previously may have its place in each of them.

## Problem-Solving Undergraduate Disciplines

In describing problem solving in a variety of academic domains, we focus first on those fields traditionally associated with the teaching of problem solving.

**Math, Science, and Engineering.** Undergraduate majors in math, the sciences, and engineering have traditionally emphasized the centrality of problem solving in their discipline. In many cases, successful problem solving in mathematics, for example, develops from the use of well-defined heuristics (Brown and Walter, 1990), which constitute the steps needed to achieve reliable and reproducible solutions. However, one should avoid the assumption that effective problem solving in these disciplines depends entirely on the mastery of particular procedures that an individual can simply choose and apply to various problems.

In many cases, students in math, science, and engineering learn a sequence of procedures known as algorithms, which they can apply to well-structured, well-defined problem situations. However, students should avoid relying on algorithms to solve entire problems and instead must realize that algorithms provide effective shortcuts in the problem-solving process (Frank, Baker, and Herron, 1987). Algorithms may prove useful for solving routine problems but not for solving entire problems in ill-defined domains (Bodner, 1987).

In an inclusive review of the literature on problem solving and the sciences, Eylon and Linn (1988) mention a number of learning habits that contribute to poor understanding of concepts in science, including the poor and imprecise use of scientific terms, a lack of understanding of causal relationships, and the belief that science involves memorization and not understanding. Alternatively, effective problem solvers in the sciences exhibit the ability to manipulate a variety of strategies, heuristics, and knowledge bases in order to solve complex problems (Woods, 1988).

One of the most effective techniques for modeling and teaching successful problem solving in math, science, and engineering remains the use of homework problems, textbooks examples, and problem-solving exercises performed by professors in front of a class (Woods, 1993). However, many students in the sciences exhibit difficulty moving beyond the basic "plug-and-chug" approaches to problem solving that depend entirely on algorithms associated with easily identified problem types (Nurrenbern and Pickering, 1987). Students eventually must learn to incorporate individual problem-solving processes in the sciences by synthesizing them with "real world" applications (Zoller, 1987). More recent innovations point to the use of computer-aided instruction in teaching undergraduates (Marcus, Cobb, and Schoenberg, 1993). Regardless of method, science and engineering educators should focus on students' interdisciplinary learning and ability to incorporate a variety of demands into their own problem-solving processes (Engineering Dean's Council and the Corporate Roundtable of the American Society for Engineering Education, 1994).

**Art and Music.** Of course, researchers in problem solving have in no way limited their inquiry to disciplines associated with the hard sciences. Studies on problem solving in art, for example, examine the cognitive processes associated with the production of creative work. In many cases, the behaviors associated with problem solving in art can be modeled and incorporated in undergraduate curricula. In a classic study, Getzels and Csikszentmihalyi (1976) found that artists essentially engage a lifelong process of solving a singular problem, a process that finds its expression in the production of successive works. The authors discovered that much of the work of problem solving in art consisted of identifying a problem, and the art school environment reinforced the formation of problem-finding behaviors by encouraging artists to interact and critique each other's maturing sense of defining artistic problems.

To adequately express the nature of artistic problems, the individual must perceive his or her own inner conflict and manifest that conflict in concrete terms in the form of a work of art (Wakefield, 1994). The process of identifying and consolidating an understanding of the problem most frequently occurs in an artist's initial attempts to conceive a final work through sketches or drawings (Dudek and Cote, 1994). In a similar sense, musicians must learn the tools for artistic expression by mastering an ability to determine such things as pitch, tone, and dissonance (McLeish, 1968). However, to produce music, individuals must not only recognize changes in music, but must also manipulate musical constructs such as pitch and tone to elicit a desired emotional response (Serafine, 1988).

**Health Professions.** Problem solving constitutes an important component in the undergraduate learning of students in the health professions. Nursing students, for example, must learn to incorporate information about patients from a variety of sources, including doctors, other nurses, patient charts, and patients' families (Johnson, Davis, and Lawbaugh, 1980). Nursing education, therefore, increasingly depends on liberal arts disciplines, which emphasize critical thinking and the ability to manipulate multiple priorities in arriving at a decision (Eisenhauer and O'Neill, 1995). Ultimately, problem solving in the health professions relies on an ability to balance uncertainty in patient care with the potential benefits and detriments associated with various treatments (Christensen and Elstein, 1991). An effective diagnosis arises from a process of generating a potential list of treatments, gathering data on a patient's health, and choosing a solution based on the collection of that data (Elstein, Shulman, and Sprafka, 1978).

**Business.** A number of authors also recommend teaching methods that encourage good problem-solving habits in business students. In business curricula, the case-study method provides an excellent tool for teaching problem solving, as students gain the opportunity to work with scenarios exhibited in actual business environments (Barnett, 1988). As in other disciplines, students learning the effective application of problem-solving techniques in business benefit tremendously from training in the liberal arts, which instill students with a sense of standards for moral behavior and encourage responsible practice in the marketplace (Pichler, 1983). This seems particularly true as students in business learn to become proficient at generating solutions, using their creativity to identify a variety of alternatives (Rubenson, 1992). Students in business classes, especially, can benefit from group interaction in problem-solving efforts, receiving critiques from their peers throughout the problem-solving process (Stinson, 1990).

The emphasis on problem-solving skills in the undergraduate curriculum has at least partially emerged from recent concern that college graduates lack the necessary skills to be successful in the modern workplace (Jones and others, 1995; Jones, Dougherty, and Fantaske, 1997). We therefore conclude the present discussion by considering how effective problem solving in undergraduate learning may translate to improved performance in the workforce.

## Moving from the Classroom to the Workplace

The need for improved problem solving derives in part from the increasingly diversified requirements of the modern workplace. Rumberger (1982) asserts that the transfer from an industrial to a service economy requires workers educated to adapt to changing technologies and increased demands for higher-order thinking skills. Well-educated workers demand greater input regarding workplace decisions, and organizations must use complex designs to retain such workers (Lawler, 1985). Organizations, in turn, should encourage their educated employees to contribute to organizational as well as individual goals, emphasizing group skills and providing an organizational climate that encourages the interdependence of workers. Employees must not only adapt to changing technologies, but also must contribute to the development of new technologies (Nash and Hawthorne, 1987). To this extent, knowledge, energy, skills, and job security facilitate workers' abilities to participate in development and team building (Morse, 1984).

Miles (1994) addresses the concerns of effective problem solving and, hence, productivity in the workplace by describing the attributes of "mindful workers." He describes the modern, "high performance" workplace in terms of changes in the management of production, the increased demand for employees who can improve their tasks as opposed to simply performing them, and the increased tendency for organizations to search outside their boundaries for assistance in solving complex problems. Professionals in acad-eme correctly assume that academic skills relate to enhanced workplace per-formance (Cappelli and Rogovsky, 1995). Most importantly, researchers and educators appear to increasingly realize the importance of teaching skills such as problem solving, critical thinking, and writing across the curriculum (Jones and others, 1995; Jones, Dougherty, and Fantaske, 1997). We should no longer view problem solving as the exclusive domain of the math, science, and engi-neering departments at undergraduate colleges and universities. Instead, research in problem solving over the past twenty years identifies the demands for effective problem-solving skills in a variety of academic domains. These skills require the creativity and facility that derives from multidisciplinary train-ing, including a broad exposure to the liberal arts, which stimulate the capac-ity for idea generation and ethical decision making required of those individuals confronted with complex, "real world" problems.

## References

Barnett, S. *Reframing and the Liberal Arts: Creative Decision-Making in the Global Marketplace.* New York: Corporate Council on the Liberal Arts, 1988.

Bloom, B. S., and Broder, J. L. *Problem-Solving Processes of College Students.* Chicago: University of Chicago Press, 1950.

Bodner, G. M. "The Role of Algorithms in Teaching Problem-Solving. *Journal of Chemical Education,* 1987, *64* (6), 513–515.

Brown, S. I., and Walter, M. I. *The Art of Problem Posing.* Hillsdale, N.J.: Erlbaum, 1990.

Cappelli, P., and Rogovsky, N. *Self-Assessed Skill Needs and Job Performance.* National Center on Adult Literacy Technical Report TR 94–08. Philadelphia: National Center on Adult Literacy, 1995.

Christensen, C., and Elstein, A. S. "Informal Reasoning in the Medical Profession." In J. F. Voss, D. N. Perkins, and J. W. Segal (eds.), *Informal Reasoning and Education.* Hillsdale, N.J.: Erlbaum, 1991.

Costa, A. L., and Lowery, L. F. *Techniques for Teaching Thinking.* Pacific Grove, Calif.: Midwest Publications, 1989.

Dudek, S. Z., and Cote, R. "Problem-Finding Revisited." In M. Runco (ed.), *Problem-Finding, Problem-Solving, and Creativity.* Norwood, N.J.: Ablex, 1994.

Eisenhauer, L. A., and O'Neill, J. A. "Synthesis and Praxis: Liberal Education and Nursing." *Liberal Education,* 1995, *81* (1), 12–17.

Elstein, A. S., Shulman, L. S., and Sprafka, S. A. *Medical Problem Solving: An Analysis of Clinical Reasoning.* Cambridge, Mass.: Harvard University Press, 1978.

Engineering Dean's Council and the Corporate Roundtable of the American Society for Engineering Education. *Engineering Education for a Changing World.* Washington, D.C.: American Society for Engineering Education, 1994.

Eylon, B., and Linn, M. C. "Learning and Instruction: An Examination of Four Research Perspectives in Science Education." *Review of Educational Research,* 1988, *58* (3), 251–301.

Frank, D. V., Baker, C. A., and Herron, J. D. "Should Students Always Use Algorithms to Solve Problems?" *Journal of Chemical Education,* 1987, *64* (6), 514–515.

Frederiksen, N. "Implications of Cognitive Theory for Instruction in Problem Solving." *Review of Educational Research,* 1984, *54,* 363–407.

Funke, J. "Solving Complex Problems: Exploration and Control of Complex Systems." In R. J. Sternberg and P. A. Frensch (eds.), *Complex Problem Solving: Principles and Mechanisms.* Hillsdale, N.J.: Erlbaum, 1991.

Getzels, J. W., and Csikszentmihalyi, M. *The Creative Vision: A Longitudinal Study of Problem Finding in Art.* New York: Wiley, 1976.

Goldenberg, E. P. "On Building Curriculum Materials That Foster Problem Posing." In S. I. Brown and M. I. Walter (eds.), *Problem Posing: Reflections and Applications.* Hillsdale, N.J.: Erlbaum, 1993.

Greenfield, L. B. "Teaching Thinking Through Problem Solving." In J. E. Stice (ed.), *Developing Critical Thinking and Problem-Solving Abilities.* New Directions for Teaching and Learning, no. 30. San Francisco: Jossey-Bass, 1987.

Harrison, A. F., and Bramson, R. M. *Styles of Thinking, Strategies for Asking Questions, Making Decisions, and Solving Problems.* Garden City, N.Y.: Anchor Press, 1982.

Hayes, J. R. "Teaching Problem-Solving Mechanisms." In D. T. Tuma and F. Reif. (eds.), *Problem Solving and Education: Issues in Teaching and Research.* Hillsdale, N.J.: Erlbaum, 1980.

Hayes, J. R. *The Complete Problem Solver.* (2nd ed.) Hillsdale, N.J.: Erlbaum, 1989.

Hegarty, M. "Knowledge and Processes in Mechanical Problem Solving." In R. A. Sternberg and P. A. Frensch (eds.), *Complex Problem Solving: Principles and Mechanisms.* Hillsdale, N.J.: Erlbaum, 1991.

Hoover, S. M., and Feldhusen, J. F. "Scientific Problem-Solving and Problem-Finding: A Theoretical Model." In M. Runco (ed.), *Problem-Finding, Problem-Solving, and Creativity.* Norwood, N.J.: Ablex, 1994.

Johnson, M. M., Davis, M. L. C., and Lawbaugh, A. M. *Problem Solving in Nursing Practice.* Dubuque, Iowa: W. C. Brown, 1980.

Jones, E. A., Dougherty, C., and Fantaske, P. *Defining Essential Critical Reading and Problem-Solving Outcomes: Perspectives of Faculty, Employers, and Policymakers.* University Park: National Center on Postsecondary Teaching, Learning, and Assessment, The Pennsylvania State University, 1997.

Jones, E. A., Hoffman, S., Melander-Moore, L., Ratcliff, G., Tibbetts, S., and Click, B.A.L., III. *National Assessment of College Student Learning: Identifying College Graduates' Essential Skills in Writing, Speech and Listening, and Critical Thinking Final Project Report.* Washington, D.C.: U.S. Department of Education, Office of Educational Research and Improvement, 1995.

Kaufmann, G. *Visual Imagery and Its Relation to Problem Solving, Theoretical and Experimental Inquiry.* Irvington-on-Hudson, N.Y.: Columbia University Press, 1979.

Kay, S. "A Method for Investigating the Creative Thought Process." In M. Runco (ed.), *Problem-Finding, Problem-Solving, and Creativity.* Norwood, N.J.: Ablex, 1994.

Kirton, M. J. "A Theory of Cognitive Style." In M. J. Kirton (ed.), *Adaptors and Innovators: Styles of Creativity in Problem-Solving.* New York: Routledge, 1989.

Lawler, E. E., III. "Education, Management Style, and Organizational Effectiveness." *Personnel Psychology,* 1985, *38* (1), 1–26.

Lesgold, A., and Lajoie, S. "Complex Problem Solving in Electronics." In R. J. Sternberg and P. A. Frensch (eds.), *Complex Problem Solving: Principles and Mechanisms.* Hillsdale, N.J.: Erlbaum, 1991.

Marcus, D., Cobb, E. B., and Schoenberg, R. E. *Lessons Learned form FIPSE Projects II.* Washington, D.C.: Fund for the Improvement of Postsecondary Education, U.S. Department of Education, 1993.

McLeish, J. *The Factor of Musical Cognition in Wing's and Seashore's Tests.* London: Novello and Company Limited, 1968.

Miles, C. *The Mindful Worker: Learning and Working into the 21st Century.* Clearwater, Fla.: H & H Publishing Company, 1994.

Morse, S. W. *Employee Educational Programs: Implications for Industry and Higher Education.* ASHE-ERIC Higher Education Research Report No. 7. Washington, D.C.: Association for the Study of Higher Education, 1984.

Nash, N. S., and Hawthorne, E. M. *Formal Recognition of Employer-Sponsored Instruction: Conflict and Collegiality in Postsecondary Education.* ASHE-ERIC Higher Education Report No. 3. Washington, D.C.: Association for the Study of Higher Education, 1987.

Newell, A., and Simon, H. A. *Human Problem Solving*. Englewood Cliffs, N.J.: Prentice Hall, 1972.

Newmann, F. M. "Higher Order Thinking in the Teaching of Social Studies: Connections Between Theory and Practice." In J. F. Voss, D. N. Perkins, and J. W. Segal (eds.), *Informal Reasoning and Education*. Hillsdale, N.J.: Erlbaum, 1991.

Norton, M., Bozeman, W. C., and Nadler, G. *Student Planned Acquisition of Required Knowledge*. Englewood Cliffs, N.J.: Educational Technology Publications, 1980.

Nurrenbern, S. C., and Pickering, M. "Concept Learning Versus Problem-Solving: Is There a Difference?" *Journal of Chemical Education*, 1987, *64* (6), 508–510.

Pichler, J. A. (1983). *Executive Values, Executive Functions, and the Humanities*. Washington, D.C.: Association of American Colleges and National Endowment for the Humanities.

Raaheim, K. *Problem Solving and Intelligence*. Bergen, Norway: Universitetsforlaget, 1974.

Rubenson, G. C. "Helping Students Evaluate Management Alternatives: The Debate." *Journal of Education for Business*, 1992, *67* (5), 287–290.

Rubinstein, M. F., and Firstenberg, I. R. "Tools for Thinking." In J. E. Stice (ed.), *Developing Critical Thinking and Problem-Solving Abilities*. New Directions for Teaching and Learning, no. 30. San Francisco: Jossey-Bass, 1987.

Rumberger, R. W. *The Structure of Work and the Underutilization of College Workers*. Stanford, Calif.: Institute for Research on Educational Finance and Governance, 1982.

Runco, M. "Conclusions Concerning Problem-Finding, Problem-Solving, and Creativity." In M. A. Runco (ed.), *Problem-Finding, Problem-Solving, and Creativity*. Norwood, N.J.: Ablex, 1994.

Serafine, M. L. *Music as Cognition: The Development of Thought in Sound*. New York: Columbia University Press, 1988.

Simon, H. A. "Information-Processing Theory of Human Problem Solving." In W. K. Estes (ed.), *Handbook of Learning and Cognitive Processes*, Vol. 5: *Human Information Processing*. Hillsdale, N.J.: Erlbaum, 1978.

Sternberg, R. J., and Horvath, J. A. "A Prototype View of Expert Teaching." *Educational Researcher*, 1995, *24* (6), 9–17.

Stinson, J. E. "Integrated Contextual Learning: Situated Learning in the Business Profession." Paper presented at the Annual Meeting of the American Educational Research Association, Boston, Mass., Apr. 16–20, 1990.

Swartz, R. J., and Perkins, D. N. *Teaching Thinking: Issues and Approaches*. Pacific Grove, Calif.: Midwest Publications, 1990.

VanGundy, A. B. *Creative Problem Solving: A Guide for Trainers and Management*. New York: Quorum Books, 1987.

Voss, J. F. "Informal Reasoning and International Relations." In J. F. Voss, D. N. Perkins, and J. W. Segal (eds.), *Informal Reasoning and Education*. Hillsdale, N.J.: Erlbaum, 1991.

Wagner, R. K. "Managerial Problem Solving," In R. J. Sternberg and P. A. Frensch. *Complex Problem Solving: Principles and Mechanisms*. Hillsdale, N.J.: Erlbaum, 1991.

Wakefield, J. F. "Problem-Finding and Empathy in Art." In M. Runco (ed.), *Problem-Finding, Problem-Solving, and Creativity*. Norwood, N.J.: Ablex, 1994.

Whimbey, A., and Lochhead, J. *Problem Solving and Comprehension*. Hillsdale, N.J.: Erlbaum, 1991.

Woods, D. R. "Novice vs. Expert Research Suggests Ideas for Implementation." *Journal of College Science Teaching*, 1988, *18* (1), 66–67, 77–79.

Woods, D. R. "PS-Where are we now?" *Journal of College Science Teaching*, 1993, *22* (5), 312–314.

Zacharakis-Jutz, J. "Adult Education, Guided Design, and Student Participation." Paper presented at the Annual Meeting of the Northern Rocky Mountain Educational Research Association, Jackson Hole, Wyo., Oct. 13–15, 1983.

Zoller, U. "The Fostering of Question-Asking Capability." *Journal of Chemical Education*, 1987, *64* (6), 510–512.

B. CHRISTOPHER DOUGHERTY is a doctoral candidate in the Higher Education Program at the Pennsylvania State University. He is currently a graduate assistant to the Director of Academic Affairs at the Pennsylvania State University's Berks Campus.

PATTI FANTASKE is a doctoral candidate and a research assistant in the Higher Education Program at the Pennsylvania State University.

*Learners and workers must be willing, not just able, to make informed, skilled, and fair-minded judgments as they solve problems, make decisions, and engage in professional practice.*

# The Motivation to Think in Working and Learning

*Peter A. Facione, Noreen C. Facione,*
*Carol Ann F. Giancarlo*

How can we habituate learners and workers to engage in thoughtful, fair-minded problem solving, decision making, and professional judgment? Demands for skillful and fair-minded thinkers arise today in every professional field and in our civic and personal lives. The pace of change accelerates, multiple sources of information saturate our senses, the rules are rewritten, and problems arise daily that defy predetermined solutions. At a minimum, to be effective learners and successful workers we must be willing and able to make informed, fair-minded judgments in contexts of relative uncertainty about what to believe and what to do in a wide variety of situations. To go beyond the minimum, workers, learners, and citizens must be willing and able to critique intelligently and amend judiciously the methods, conceptualizations, contexts, evidence, and standards applied in any given problem situation. In short, we must habitually, not just skillfully, engage in critical thinking in a world that is so dynamic that today's verities are yesterdays misconceptions. Thus, the driving question is, how is the consistent internal motivation to think critically identified, measured, and nurtured?

As the twentieth century ends, uncertain world economic conditions and dynamic social realities reveal that strong thinking skills and solid content knowledge are essential but not sufficient (Marshall and Tucker, 1992). We must prepare graduates who have the motivating habits of mind to be willing, if not eager, to engage in thinking. They must ask tough and challenging questions, they must be alert to potential problems, they must be judicious in making decisions, and they must be mentally oriented toward following reasons and evidence wherever they may lead. The challenge for educators and mentors is to identify, measure, and motivate thoughtful, fair-minded engagement in problem solving, decision making, and professional judgment. The challenge is, in short, to prepare graduates both able and willing to think.

## Habits of Mind

The familiar contrast between habits and skills is evident in the case of healthful living. One habituated to healthful living is more likely to exercise, eat right, practice preventive health, avoid risky activities (such as smoking or unsafe sex), and the like. Another might have the beliefs and skill to engage in the same healthful life style, but not habitually do so. That person, we would say, is not so disposed. The same is true for thinking. People may have the skill to think well and the topic knowledge to deal with a given problem, and yet, unless it is demanded of them by some external force, they may not engage the problem and apply their skills and knowledge. These people do not have a strong disposition toward critical thinking; they are not internally motivated to use thinking as their main problem-solving strategy. Just as we expect the person disposed toward healthful living generally to engage in what are believed to be healthful practices, we expect one disposed toward critical thinking generally to apply the skills of analysis, interpretation, inference, explanation, evaluation, and self-correction to the problem, decision, or judgment situation at hand.

Smokers who have tried to break that habit know well how easily some habits are formed and how difficult they can be to break. Forming habits, good or bad, often begins with actions performed because of external motivations, such as compliance with rules or conformity to the social norm. The seedling habit begins its tender growth nurtured by positive reinforcement for early, even if modest, successes. Failures and backsliding can be overcome by taking up the requisite practices again after each setback. Often a combination of internal and external motivators facilitate this, as any patient parent, supervisor, coach, mentor, counselor, or educator will attest. In theory, over time the motivation to engage in the behaviors associated with the habit becomes more consistent and internalized, and the habit takes root in our personalities.

Seven positive aspects of the disposition toward critical thinking in students and workers are the consistent internal motivations to be inquisitive, organized, analytical, confident, judicious, tolerant, and intellectually honest. We could express these same seven in terms of such things as being curious about how things work; systematically persisting even when the matter at hand is difficult; being alert to problem situations and potential difficulties; being appropriately trustful of one's own ability to reason and make sound decisions; seeing that there are times when decisions need to be made, revised, or deferred; being open-minded about other approaches or new ideas; and asking tough but important questions, particularly when it means pursuing reasons and following evidence wherever they may lead. When strong dispositions toward critical thinking are absent, people can demonstrate negative dispositions such as ambivalence or even hostility toward resolving problem situations through reason.

The overall disposition toward critical thinking is the consistent internal motivation to employ one's critical thinking abilities in judging what to believe or to do in any situation. If one is inclined or disposed toward thoughtful and intellectually honest problem solving, and if one is also skilled and knowledgeable, there is a much greater chance that one will be consistently successful. The higher the stakes of the situation and the more likely that potential problems will be unexpected and ill-defined, the more significant these thinking dispositions become. The Secret Service rotates experienced agents off of presidential security duty every few months to be sure that the analytic vigilance of those guarding the president does not wane due to the routine of the job. The U.S. Air Force Academy, where the preparation of combat-ready military officers is a priority, built thinking dispositions like inquisitiveness and judiciousness into the educational outcomes performance standards alongside leadership development and problem-solving skills (U.S. Air Force Academy, 1995). In nursing and other health care professions, where life or death may depend on the problem solving done in an emergency situation or on the interpretations of subtle changes in a recovering patient's status, critical thinking is a mandatory outcome in professional school accreditation (National League for Nursing, 1990).

## The Science and Application of the Disposition Toward Critical Thinking

Philosophical speculations and educational theories about the dispositional side of thinking can be traced back to the ancient Greeks. The rationale for a classical liberal education advanced in the nineteenth century at many American colleges was hardly the Renaissance notion of learning for its own sake, but rather the practical concern, often driven by the religiosity of the era, for character development through mental and physical discipline. By the first third of the twentieth century, American higher education, with its land grant universities, was abandoning the classical liberal arts in favor of more commercially useful curricula (Boyer, 1994). Important figures in American intellectual life, such as John Dewey, continued to emphasize the development of thinking skills and dispositions as a cornerstone of democratic society (Dewey, 1933). Although the echo of Dewey's concern was sometimes heard, it was all but obliterated during the middle and later decades of the century, as comprehensive universities and research universities devalued the baccalaureate core in favor of departmental majors. However, interest in thinking dispositions reemerged, as educators in professional programs, sensing the limitation of the narrowly specialized skills-only approach, began exploring broader conceptualizations of problem solving and encountered colleagues in the liberal arts who sought to connect their work on teaching for thinking with content-rich professional fields. Today, one finds a growing number of conceptualizations of the dispositional side of critical thinking, some speculative (Ennis, 1987; Kurfiss, 1988; Siegel, 1988; Paul, 1990; Perkins, 1993) and others more empirically based (P. A. Facione, 1990a; Jones, 1993; Wade and Tavris, 1993; P. A. Facione, Giancarlo (Sanchez), N. C. Facione, and Gainen (Kurfiss), 1995; King and Kitchener, 1994).

Empirical research on critical thinking and its dispositional component began when theoreticians, eager to get on with the business of measuring critical thinking, wearied of dulling, detailed, definitional diatribes and dogmatic, data-less dog-and-pony, didactic displays. Many felt that there was sufficient agreement about core ideas to move forward. Professional schools and their associations, desiring to measure the learning outcomes of preparation programs, required workable assessment strategies (National League for Nursing, 1990; Gainen and Locatelli, 1995). Then, when the U.S. Congress made critical thinking an outcome for college graduates in the *Goals 2000* act (U.S. Congress, 1994), many wondered whether critical thinking could ever be defined well enough to permit an inquiry as to whether and to what extent this goal was being achieved (U.S. Department of Education, 1993).

Fortunately, theoreticians were already working toward a consensus conceptualization. In 1990, after a two-year process, an expert consensus statement defined critical thinking in a broadly applicable, nontechnical way. *Critical thinking is purposeful self-regulatory judgment;* that is, a decision about what to do or to believe that was open to one's own review and revision. In coming to that judgment one gives *reasoned consideration to evidence, methods, conceptualizations, contexts, and standards.* The core skills one uses interactively in this process include interpretation, analysis, inference, evaluation, explanation, and self-regulation (P. A. Facione, 1990a). Insisting that critical thinkers are persons, the experts participating in this Delphi project developed a detailed characterization of the dispositional features of the ideal critical thinker.

Independent empirical confirmation of the basic consensus concept of critical thinking came in interesting ways. Using previously extant testing tools and factor analytic methods, Taube (forthcoming) verified that critical thinking had both a dispositional and a skill dimension. The list of specific core critical thinking skills and sub-skills was independently ratified by a research project sponsored by the U.S. Department of Education, using survey data gathered from college faculty, employers, and policy makers. This study, originally conceived as addressing only skills, added a listing of dispositional attributes to its survey tool. There was virtual unanimity in the enthusiastic endorsement of these dispositional elements (Jones and others, 1994).

The first tool to reliably measure the disposition toward critical thinking built on the 1990 Delphi study expert consensus description of the ideal critical thinker. *The California Critical Thinking Disposition Inventory (CCTDI)* measures the strength of a person's disposition toward or away from critical thinking (P. A. Facione and N. C. Facione, 1992; P. A. Facione, N. C. Facione, and Giancarlo (Sanchez), 1994). Given that the disposition toward critical thinking is its motivational component, the development of the CCTDI used established psychological testing strategies. The CCTDI measures the disposition globally and in seven aspects, described later in this section. It reports a total score ranging from 70 to 420, with 280 or higher indicating a positive overall disposition toward critical thinking. Each of the seven aspect scales range from 10 to 60, with a positive score being 40 or higher. Scale scores below 35 suggest negative dispositional characteristics, such as intolerance, imprudence, lack of confidence, or disregard for relevant reasons and evidence.

Workplace and classroom application of the seven CCTDI scales is easy to grasp if one imagines someone negatively disposed on a given scale. *Truth-seeking* measures intellectual honesty, the courageous desire for best knowledge in any situation, the inclination to ask challenging questions and to follow the reasons and evidence wherever they lead. How many managers have failed their companies by shying away from the hard questions, discounting important but unpleasant data, and preferring outmoded ways of doing business or untested assumptions about the marketplace?

*Open-mindedness* measures tolerance for new ideas and divergent views. What are the chances of helpful critique or innovation if one is intolerant and closed-minded?

*Systematicity* measures the inclination to be organized, focused, diligent, and persevering. How much business will be lost by a customer service representative whose approach to clients is disorganized, unfocused, sloppy, and half-hearted?

*Inquisitiveness* measures intellectual curiosity and the intention to learn things even if their immediate application is not apparent. Workers who are indifferent or disdainful of learning more than the minimum necessary to get through the day's tasks should not expect frequent and speedy promotions.

*Analyticity* measures alertness to potential difficulties and awareness of the need to intervene by the use of reason and evidence to solve problems. A health care professional, an attorney, a teacher, a manager, an engineer, or a policymaker who is not inclined toward analyticity will likely fail to anticipate significant consequences and, thereby, increase the risk of malpractice and negligence.

*Cognitive maturity* measures judiciousness, which inclines one to see the complexity in problems and to desire prudent decision making. Those who see everything as starkly good or bad, right or wrong, true or false are unlikely to be sophisticated learners or good candidates for positions of increasing responsibility. They are apt to make decisions too hastily or too slowly; to be unwilling to reconsider; to be dogmatic and dualistic, if not outright simplistic, in their approach to problem-solving; and to lack sensitivity to the nuances of circumstances and subtleties of context.

*Critical thinking self-confidence* measures trust in one's own reasoning and ability to guide others to make rational decisions. A career involving thoughtful decision making or mediative problem solving is not encouraged for persons weak in reasoning self-confidence. If one's reasoning self-confidence is founded on strong critical thinking skills and the disposition to use them, one can become successful in a wide variety of executive, managerial, client service, and professional occupations.

Personality research and concurrent validity studies of the disposition toward critical thinking are ways of connecting critical thinking, with its humanistic roots, to scientific knowledge. For example, the 1990 Delphi consensus description of the ideal critical thinker was tested by Giancarlo (1996a) using the California $Q$ sort (Block, 1961). Twenty nationally recognized experts in adult critical thinking individually sorted the one hundred $Q$ sort items so that the result would characterize, in their opinions, the ideal critical thinker. The twenty were merged to form a prototype personality profile of the ideal critical thinker ($r = .80$, $N = 20$, $p < .001$). This prototype correlated with undergraduate students' CCTDI scores ($r = .36$, $N = 91$, $p < .001$) and with CCTDI and $Q$ sort data collected about those students from their peers ($r = .32$, $N = 91$, $p < .001$). This finding confirms the strength of the 1990 consensus description of the ideal critical thinker and supports the validity of measurement tools based on that definition.

Seeking further connections between the disposition toward critical thinking and better established personality constructs, Giancarlo explored ego-resilience—an indication of one's psychological flexibility, mental health, and adjustment—(Block, 1965; Block and Block, 1980), and openness to experience—an indication of engagement with one's environment, curiosity, and diligence (Costa and McCrae, 1992). The disposition toward critical thinking, as measured on the CCTDI, is positively correlated with ego-resilience ($r = .58$, $N = 198$, $p < .001$) and openness to experience ($r = .37$, $N = 198$, $p < .001$). This suggests that those scoring higher on the CCTDI are more likely to be engaged in their environment, focused, diligent, objective, intellectually curious, and psychologically flexible and healthy—certainly a desirable combination of personality characteristics from the perspective of the workplace as well as the classroom.

Assessing the critical thinking process is a challenge if the only available data is the product of that thinking. From the product alone, it is difficult to ascertain the skills and dispositions that went into the thinking process. But if raters are able to observe learners or workers engaged in the process of doing their tasks, and if those learners or workers are able to articulate what they are thinking as they go along, scoring rubrics and rating forms can be applied with considerable success. Within a reasonably brief period of time people can become adept at making reliable and valid judgments about the relative ranking of different workers or learners on such scales. As raters and those being rated internalize the language of critical thinking, they become better able to communicate about how to improve decision making.

Combining multiple measures of thinking, gathered systematically and evaluated reliably, creates assessment portfolios. Properly used, these can provide valuable information to teachers and mentors about the progress, strengths, and weaknesses of learners and workers, particularly in professional settings (N. C. Facione and P. A. Facione, 1996a).

Holistic strategies to assess the dispositional side of critical thinking use tools that mix skill measurement with dispositional measurement. These kinds of tools offer more qualitative data but sacrifice precision. *The Holistic Critical Thinking Scoring Rubric* is in the public domain and available on the World Wide Web at http://www.calpress.com (P. A. Facione and N. C. Facione, 1994). Adaptations to the workplace yield rating forms such as the *Professional Judgment Rating Form: Novice/Internship Level* (N. C. Facione and P. A. Facione, 1996b). The U.S. Air Force Academy incorporated the language of critical thinking dispositions in developing a rating system in its report, "Levels of Performance for Framing and Resolving Ill-Defined Problems" (U.S. Air Force Academy, 1995). Work with fieldwork supervisors and employers for hundreds of human services and accounting internship settings in the Los Angeles area led to detailed evaluation checklists for written communication, speech communication, and critical thinking (Carter-Wells, 1995). As we watch people engaged in the process of problem solving we can, with practice, reliably discern the habits of mind that they bring to the endeavor, not just their skill and content knowledge in working through the problem at hand.

Some philosophers have suggested using multiple-choice or multiple-rating skill test items as an indirect measure of thinking dispositions. One might hypothesize that a closed-minded, unsystematic, or inattentive test taker would be more likely to select a given wrong answer on a multiple-choice skills test than to reason his or her way to the right answer (P. A. Facione, 1990b). For example, *The California Critical Thinking Skills Test (CCTST),* a multiple-choice instrument, was designed so that some wrong answer choices are more likely to distract persons with weak or negative thinking dispositions (P. A. Facione, 1990c).

As valid as it may be for the measurement of skills, the CCTST is not a test of dispositions. Skills tests can and should be evaluated on appropriate criteria relating to their feasibility and validity as skills tests (Pendarvis, 1996). However, we do not recommend using skills tests to measure dispositional attributes. It is implausible to suppose that one can reliably evaluate the specific motivation behind the thinking process if one's only data point is the product that the process produced. It is unreasonable to draw firm conclusions about why a given person selected a given wrong answer from the mere fact that the person marked a particular choice on a test of thinking skills. Unless perhaps augmented by simultaneous talk-aloud data, we would not know whether the person selected the wrong answer because of weak analytical or inference skills, a misinterpretation of the prompt or answer choices, an incorrect evaluation of those choices, an incorrect guess, distraction caused by weak dispositions, or something else entirely such as simply having mismarked the scoring sheet. To discern reliably whether or not a person is deeply motivated in a certain way requires scales of far higher alpha reliability than can possibly be obtained using a single response to a single item. Objective tools built on sound psychological measurement principles can yield valid and reliable information about a person's consistent motivation toward critical thinking without risking the many pitfalls associated with using skills test items.

## Early Findings from College Studies

Studies of junior high, high school, and graduate school students are taking place in several countries using native language versions of the CCTDI (Giancarlo and Facione, 1994; Ferguson and Vazquez-Abad, 1995; McBride, 1995; Chang, 1996; Giancarlo 1996b; Mancinelli, 1996). Although these schools produce people entering the workforce, space constraints dictate only a quick look at early college level longitudinal and cross-sectional studies (Facione, P. A., Giancarlo [Sanchez], C. A., and Facione, N. C., 1994). In the fall of 1992 we profiled entering freshmen at a selective, private, comprehensive, liberal arts–oriented American university on the day before classes started in September (P. A. Facione, Giancarlo [Sanchez], N. C. Facione, and Gainen [Kurfiss] 1995). We tested those students as graduating seniors in April and May 1996, capturing data on 154 students at both ends of their undergraduate careers. The overall score grew from an initially positive pretest mean of 303.4 to a posttest mean of 310.8. Matching students' 1992 freshman year scores with their own 1996 senior year score showed a statistically significant positive increase in their disposition toward critical thinking ($t = 3.244$, $p < .001$). Statistically significant growth occurred in truth-seeking, where the 1992 score was a disappointing 36.1, and the 1996 score landed in the neutral zone at 38.9 ($t = 5.7$, $p < .001$). In all the studies with which we are familiar, the consistently substandard truth-seeking—intellectual honesty—mean scores are worrisome indicators of serious weakness in this specific and crucially important aspect of the disposition. The other statistically significant growth occurred in reasoning self-confidence ($t = 4.39$, $p < .001$), which, as with the other five scales, showed mean scores above 40 on the pretest and posttest.

More encouraging than the growth was the strong correlation ($r = .55$, $p < .001$) between the college students' 1992 freshman pretest scores and their 1996 senior scores. This is the first documented evidence suggesting that the overall disposition toward critical thinking appears to be stable over a period of years, but there is room for significant growth.

Professional schools, including graduate and undergraduate programs in nursing, engineering, communication, management, pharmacy, military science, and education, desiring to measure the critical thinking skills and disposition of exiting students, have begun exploring the use of quantitative and qualitative measures. The nursing profession is the most advanced at this time in both the conceptualization of the relationship between critical thinking and the ways of reasoning (Fonteyn, forthcoming) as described by experienced practitioners and in terms of learning outcomes assessment and program development. Now completing the second round, our Nursing Meta-Study of undergraduate and graduate nursing students is receiving critical thinking test score data from 90 participating universities and colleges throughout the United States. The results, which will be considered in relation to institutional variables as well as more traditional indicators of student academic data and licensure rates, will be published in 1997.

# Recommendations for the Workplace and the Classroom

People able and willing to make thoughtful, purposeful judgments will come from environments that nurture thinking and reflective problem solving more than automatic or scripted problem solving. Within business as well as schools and homes the cultivation of a culture that encourages thinking and honest inquiry is essential. Mentors and educators in every professional field and academic discipline can guide workers and students to use their thinking skills more effectively and become more motivated toward thinking without compromising content knowledge. It is not unreasonable to hypothesize that a stronger motivation toward critical thinking would actually increase the potential for content knowledge acquisition. The fundamental strategy for mentor and educator alike is to balance nurture with challenge while directing the learner toward the next most achievable area for development. Those of us working on how to nurture the disposition toward critical thinking recommend five things.

**One: Cultivate a Culture of Reasoned Thinking and Evidence-Based Inquiry.** Leaders must model those habits of mind and use those thinking skills that others are expected to emulate and exercise. Every element in an organization, from personnel practices to client services and product quality, must be scrutinized to determine whether its practices and policies enhance or inhibit thinking. Whereas scripted or rote procedures are efficient responses to predictable problems, leaders must not be so recipe-bound that others are prevented by the hostility of the working environment from fully exercising their critical thinking skills and habits of mind. Not every problem can be anticipated and script-solved, not every innovation will come from the top. A corporate culture that encourages creative and critical thinking not only reflects the confidence leadership has in the vigor and viability of the enterprise, it invites the kind of employee loyalty that yields high-quality effort and innovative solutions.

**Two: Replace Rote Training with Thoughtful Mentoring.** The workplace and the classroom can be bridged not only by comparable learning experiences, but by teaching and assessment expectations that focus on outcomes. Mentors and instructors must abandon rote training and memorization of scripted routines to achieve genuine education. Education in content-heavy domains requires reflection on experience wherein the crucial scripts are made understandable at a level that permits the practitioner to execute the recipe; to understand the rationale for each step; and to adapt, revise, or discard the script in appropriate situations. Education is learning to know whether and why, not just what, how, and when. As uncomfortable as this may be for some learners who think that good teaching is telling exactly what will be on the test, the development of professional, disciplined practice demands more. Sophisticated evaluators of effective teaching understand how to interpret students' comments in light of students' levels of appreciation for what good teaching really means. Challenging students to think includes asking probing questions, demanding understandable explanations, questioning untested assumptions, and, at times, letting people make mistakes that they can then fix themselves. Self-correction is the point of meta-cognition. An instructor or mentor can mix nurture with challenge and can point the way toward learning by helping learners to see relevant patterns in apparently chaotic information and to identify promising approaches to problems. However, the person who guides learning should never spoon-feed solutions or accept right answers wrongly understood. The effective mentor does not become a codependent. Responsibility for learning is the learner's.

**Three: Present Information from the Bottom Up.** Corporations and professions, like academic disciplines, are digests of theories, methods, rules, and standards to be applied to a given range of questions in a given set of circumstances to produce an expected set of results. But how we construct and package that knowledge is often the opposite from how we learn it. For most people, learning on the job or in school starts with the particular, not the general. To take advantage of this, instructors and mentors should not begin with first principles and basic definitions, but with examples that are so engaging that learners are eager to acquire the targeted content and skills. Thus motivated, the learners will then seek definitions and principles as aids to organize their growing bodies of new knowledge. Sequenced examples and assignments can draw on an ever greater content base and more sophisticated understandings of previous content. The case study approach, like problem-based learning, offers many advantages. Whether practiced in the workplace or the classroom, the analysis of cases representing the best and the worst of professional practice offers sufficient concreteness to engage learners, whether experts or novices. Case studies integrate content, skills, and dispositions in ways that are authentic relative to professional practice. Because they are memorably concrete, they can easily be called to mind when their lessons require reinforcement.

Too often, when working cases or using other teaching strategies, we show our students and new colleagues the product of our work and not the processes through which it was accomplished (Kurfiss, 1988). Modeling thoughtfulness means showing, among other things, what it is to think through a problem and make decisions. It can be better not to rehearse what one wants to demonstrate in order to permit one's more spontaneous and authentic thinking to be revealed. Encouraging students to voice their thinking as well, by talking aloud as they work through a problem, can reveal crucial elements in their thinking process or habits of mind, which can then be explored, reinforced, or amended.

**Four: Evaluate Processes, Not Only Results.** When concerned about content knowledge and automatic or scripted problem solving, we can look primarily, if not exclusively, at the results to evaluate the worker or student. We have the product we can evaluate or the completed essay we can grade. But to build thinking skills and strengthen thinking dispositions, mentors and educators must look to the process. It is not enough to get the right answer; one must be able to get to that answer by solid reasoning. The right result achieved for the wrong reason could be a lucky thing one time and a disaster for clients and company alike the next. Educators and mentors can get at the process of thinking by encouraging learners to keep reflective logs of striking examples of excellent or terrible thinking, by making a videotape of classroom presentations or actual services to clients to permit reflective analysis at a later time, or by using talk-aloud strategies to externalize thinking. Using qualitative performance rubrics that integrate the habits of mind with the thinking skills, and sharing these rubrics with learners during the instructional process, helps learners to internalize the standards of evaluation and reinforces the significance of the thinking process for them. What is measured is valued.

**Five: Expect and Reward Virtue.** The consistent internal motivation to be inquisitive, organized, analytical, confident, judicious, tolerant, and intellectually honest is an intellectual virtue. This virtue inclines us toward being learners our whole lives and toward being thoughtful, engaged, and effective problem solvers and decision makers in our jobs and professions. Workers and learners should be advised that the expectations go well beyond memorizing for the final exam or moving one's mail from the in-basket to the out-basket. Although some might think that virtue is its own reward, it need not be its only reward. Employers and educators looking for qualitatively superior work rather than compliant minimalist performances would do well to assure that rewards, resources, and reinforcement flow to those who are able and willing to think.

# References

Block, J. *The Q-Sort Method in Personality Assessment and Psychiatric Research.* Palo Alto, Calif.: Consulting Psychologists Press, 1961.

Block, J. *The Challenge of Response Sets: Unconfounding Meaning, Acquiescence, and Social Desirability in the MMPI.* New York: Appleton-Century-Crofts, 1965.

Block, J. H., and Block, J. "The Role of Ego-Control and Ego-Resilience in the Organization of Behavior." In W.A. Collins (ed.), *Development of Cognition, Affect, and Social Relations.* Hillsdale, N.J.: Erlbaum, 1980.

Boyer, E. L. *The Student as Scholar: Reflections on the Future of Liberal Learning.* Cambridge, Mass.: Academy of Arts and Sciences, 1994.

Carter-Wells, J. "Job Skills Analysis Strategies." Presentation at the American Association of Higher Education Assessment Forum, Boston, 1995.

Chang, L. "Critical Thinking Disposition and Preferred Teaching Strategies of Students in a Two- and a Five-Year Associate Degree Nursing Program in Taiwan, Republic of China." Unpublished doctoral dissertation, School of Nursing, University of Maryland, 1996.

Costa, P. T., Jr., and McCrae, R. R. *The Revised NEO Personality Inventory: Professional Manual.* Odessa, Fla.: Psychological Assessment Resources, 1992.

Dewey, J. *How We Think.* Lexington, Mass.: Heath, 1933.

Ennis, R. "A Taxonomy of Critical Thinking Dispositions and Abilities." In J. Barton and R. Sternberg (ed.), *Teaching Thinking Skills.* New York: Freeman, 1987.

Facione, N. C., and Facione, P. A. "Assessment Design Issues for Evaluating Critical Thinking in Nursing." *Holistic Nursing Practice,* 1996a, *10* (3), 44–51

Facione, N. C., and Facione, P. A. *Professional Judgment Rating Form: Novice/Internship Level.* Millbrae: California Academic Press, 1996b.

Facione, P. A. *Critical Thinking: A Statement of Expert Consensus for Purposes of Educational Assessment and Instruction.* 1990a. (ED 315 423)

Facione, P. A. *Interpreting the CCTST, Group Norms, and Sub-scores.* CCTST Technical Report no. 4. 1990b. (ED 327 566)

Facione, P. A. *The California Critical Thinking Skills Test and Manual.* Millbrae: California Academic Press, 1990c.

Facione, P. A., and Facione, N. C. *The California Critical Thinking Disposition Inventory.* Millbrae: California Academic Press, 1992.

Facione, P. A., and Facione, N. C. *The Holistic Critical Thinking Scoring Rubric.* Millbrae: California Academic Press, 1994.

Facione, P. A., Facione N. C., and Giancarlo (Sanchez), C. A. "Critical Thinking Disposition as a Measure of Competent Clinical Judgment: The Development of the California Critical Thinking Disposition Inventory." *Journal of Nursing Education,* 1994, *33,* 345–350.

Facione, P. A., Giancarlo (Sanchez), C. A., and Facione, N. C. "Are College Students Disposed to Think?" Paper presented at the Sixth International Conference on Thinking, Boston, July 1994. (ED 368 311)

Facione, P. A., Giancarlo (Sanchez), C. A., Facione, N. C., and Gainen (Kurfiss), J. "The Disposition Toward Critical Thinking. "*Journal of General Education,* 1995, *44* (1), 1–25.

Ferguson, N., and Vazquez-Abad, J. "An Exploration of the Interplay of Students' Disposition to Critical Thinking, Formal Thinking, and Procedural Knowledge in Science." Postdissertation paper, University of Montreal, 1995.

Fonteyn, M. *Thinking Strategies for Critical Practice,* Philadelphia: Lippincott, forthcoming.

Gainen (Kurfiss), J., and Locatelli, P. *Assessment for the New Curriculum: A Guide for Professional Accounting Programs.* Sarasota, Fla.: American Accounting Association, 1995.

Giancarlo, C. A. "The Ideal Critical Thinker: Development of an Expert Q-Sort Prototype," Presented at the American Psychological Association Meeting, Toronto, Canada, 1996a.

Giancarlo, C. A. *Critical Thinking, Culture and Personality: Predicting Latinos' Academic Success.* Unpublished doctoral dissertation, Department of Psychology, University of California at Riverside, 1996b.

Giancarlo, C. A., and Facione, N. C. *A Study of the Critical Thinking Disposition and Skill of Spanish and English Speaking Students at Camelback High School.* Millbrae: California Academic Press, 1994.

Jones, E. A. *Critical Thinking Literature Review.* University Park: The National Center for Postsecondary Teaching, Learning and Assessment, The Pennsylvania State University, 1993.

Jones, E. A., Hoffman, S., Melander-Moore, L., Ratcliff, G., Tibbetts, S., and Click, B.A.L. *Essential Skills in Writing, Speech and Listening, and Critical Thinking for College Graduates: Perspectives of Faculty, Employers, and Policy Makers.* Project summary, U.S. Department of Education, OERI Contract No. R117G10037. University Park: National Center for Postsecondary Teaching, Learning and Assessment, The Pennsylvania State University, 1994.

King, P. M., and Kitchener, K. S. *Developing Reflective Judgment: Understanding and Promoting Intellectual Growth and Critical Thinking in Adolescents and Adults.* San Francisco: Jossey-Bass, 1994.

Kurfiss (Gainen), J. *Critical Thinking: Theory, Research, Practice, and Possibilities.* ASHE-ERIC Higher Education Report No. 2. Washington D.C.: ASHE, 1988.

Mancinelli, I. "The Role of Critical Thinking and Economic Advances of Mexican Americans in Corporate America." Unpublished doctoral dissertation, Department of Psychology, Saybrook Institute, 1996.

Marshall, R., and Tucker, M. *Thinking for a Living.* New York: Basic Books, 1992.

McBride, R. Personal correspondence, College of Education, Texas A&M University, 1995.

National League for Nursing. *Accreditation Standards for Baccalaureate Degree Programs and Master's Degree Programs.* New York: National League for Nursing, 1990.

Paul, R. *Critical Thinking.* Rohnert Park, Calif.: Sonoma State University Center for Critical Thinking and Moral Critique, 1990.

Pendarvis, F. *Critical Thinking Assessment: Measuring a Moving Target.* Rock Hill: South Carolina Higher Education Assessment Network, 1996.

Perkins, D., Jay, E., and Tishman, S. "Beyond Abilities: A Dispositional Theory of Thinking." *Merrill-Palmer Quarterly,* 1993, *39* (1), 1–21.

Siegel, H. *Educating Reason.* New York: Routledge, 1988.

Taube, K. T., "Critical Thinking Ability and Disposition as Factors of Performance on a Written Critical Thinking Test." *Journal of General Education,* forthcoming.

U.S. Air Force Academy. *Phase 1: Final Report of the USAFA Educational Outcomes Assessment Working Group.* Colorado Springs, Colo.: United States Air Force Academy, 1995.

U.S. Congress. *Goals 2000: National Goals for Education Act.* Washington, D.C.: Government Printing Office, 1994.

U.S. Department of Education. *National Assessment of College Student Learning: Getting Started.* Washington, D.C.: U.S. Department of Education, 1993.

Wade, C., and Tavris, C. *Psychology.* (3rd ed.) New York: Harper, 1993.

*PETER A. FACIONE serves as dean of the College of Arts and Sciences and administrator of the Division of Counseling Psychology and Education at Santa Clara University.*

*NOREEN C. FACIONE researches help seeking for breast cancer in minority populations through the Department of Physiological Nursing at the University of California at San Francisco.*

*CAROL ANN F. GIANCARLO researches the relationship between critical thinking, academic success, and cultural variables through the Department of Psychology at Santa Clara University.*

*This chapter discusses how to make technology investments that pay off for colleges and universities in terms of program quality, faculty renewal, and graduate employability.*

# Using Technology to Enhance Students' Skills

*Ann Deden, Vicki K. Carter*

What pedagogical imperatives drive colleges and universities to incorporate computer technologies into their curricula? At least five forces drive this change. First, information access by means of the World Wide Web is becoming more important for student research, because it can provide quick access to primary sources of information, including researchers themselves. Students as well as faculty need this tool in order to gain access to the mushrooming amounts of information only available electronically. With the advent of the Web, new standards for up-to-date information and new access to the debates that shape our thinking require participation in knowledge formation as part of modern society. The concomitant acceleration in the rate of job change requires skillful use of information tools for lifelong learning.

Second, computer-based simulations offer a level of realism and heightened potential to apply college learning to on-the-job performance. From lab simulations in biology, chemistry, and physics to election simulations in the social sciences, these powerful tools help students learn both course content and problem-solving skills that make them more effective learners and employees.

Third, new communications skills, such as intercultural e-mail etiquette and nonlinear multimedia document creation, are being emphasized by employers as prerequisites for employment. While many colleges resist seeing themselves as vocational schools, all are increasingly pressured to produce tangible results in terms of employable graduates, especially as tuition costs continue to rise.

Fourth, computer technology can provide asynchronous learning that meets the needs of working and nontraditional students by removing location and time barriers. Equal access to information is close to being considered a constitutionally guaranteed right. Also, to the extent that electronic access supplants physical access, computer technology can increase enrollments without increasing physical plant construction. It can also give a larger, more geographically dispersed student body access to specialists and top instructors not available locally.

Fifth, pedagogical improvement and faculty renewal can be both stimulated and supported by these technologies. In the classroom, faculty quickly take advantage of technology to reduce the length of lectures, relate lecture content and abstract concepts to concrete realities, and provide hands-on learning experiences. Beyond the classroom, faculty use asynchronous communications technologies to extend discussion, mentoring, and coaching; to add richer practice exercises; and to provide more timely and individualized feedback.

Additional motivators include market share and the cost of new construction. These factors directly affect the financial viability of the institution. The potential for distributed education offered by the new media remove geographical boundaries to competition for students. Institutions are jockeying for position as competition for the nontraditional learner—especially worksite-based education—heats up.

One clear early winner in the competition is Maricopa County Community College District (MCCD) in Phoenix, Arizona. MCCD has had a strategic plan in place since 1994 that uses computer technology to "enhance the creation of student-centered learning environment" ("Maricopa County Community College District Governing Board," 1994).

The MCCD's Web page explains that, as a result of investments in the technology and people needed to achieve this vision, "the Maricopa Community Colleges rank among the nation's leading institutions of higher education in the use of computers and telecommunications. Computer-related courses number close to 600." MCCD has used technology to strengthen its ability to achieve its primary mission and to reach more of its target audience. Eighty percent of its students are employed adults. Partly because of technology-supported ease of access, area employers enroll more than 19,700 employees in MCCD courses each year. Sixty-four percent of the upper division enrollment at neighboring Arizona State University now comes from MCCD.

Another outstanding example is the Dallas Community College District's Global Learning Network and OLLIE (On Line Learning, Interaction, and Exchange) system ("On Line Learning, Interaction, and Exchange," 1996). Although it is not as fully developed as Maricopa's system, DCCD is clearly moving in the direction of what some have called the *virtual university*. Programs like these take advantage of technology to collapse the distinction between residential and distance education and to improve learning access for all students.

As the cost of new construction continues to rise, opportunities to increase enrollments without building more classrooms and dormitories become increasingly attractive. Many institutions are redirecting their infrastructure investments away from brick and mortar to "wire"—making Internet and intranet connectivity available from every dorm room and every classroom and office desk.

Thomas W. West, associate vice chancellor for information resources and technology of the California State University, argues (1996) that

> over time a network infrastructure will be demonstrably less expensive than building and maintaining a traditional campus physical plant. For instance, we estimate that it would take $750 million of capital funds to construct a new campus for 15,000 students. For the same amount we can build out the networking infrastructure of our 22 campuses and provide a network with sufficient bandwidth to handle the interactive video, high speed data and voice necessary to share instruction and information resources. To accomplish this trade-off we would need to have an average 5 percent increase in each campus's enrollment within existing resources.

When an argument this persuasive can be made, expanding enrollment by means of technologically distributed education becomes a very attractive alternative.

## Challenges Associated with New Technologies

Opportunities for information access, computer-based simulations, development of job-relevant communications skills, asynchronous learning, faculty renewal, increased market share, and reduced construction costs may make technology appear to be the solution to all of education's ills. However, investment in technology does not guarantee that any of these benefits will be realized. A number of factors can cause institutional technology initiatives to fall short of success. This failure may happen through lack of integration with other reforms. It can also occur when administrators and faculty expect outcomes the technology does not produce.

In the remainder of this chapter, we will examine potential pitfalls and contrast them with examples of the successes that can be achieved with appropriate use of technology. Finally, we will discuss strategies for making the transition to a more powerful learning infrastructure.

Lack of a pedagogical rationale and focus is the first potential threat to significant program outcomes. Some institutions assume that merely having the technology available is enough; faculty and students will figure out the best ways to use it. This approach typically produces underutilization of the technology's potential as a tool for instructional improvement. Symptoms include spotty adoption patterns and the use of technology merely to enrich lectures. Typically, one or two instructors per department use the lion's share of the technology resources to create multimedia lecture illustrations, computerized slide presentations, or Web pages that are compendiums of information without defined instructional applicability.

Although in the long term faculty might evolve technology applications that contribute greatly to significant learning outcomes, it is more productive to accelerate their process. Competition for market share and the rate of technological change require quicker uptake and more efficient, effective use of the technology to pay back the institution's investment.

Ineffective technology adoption also occurs when institutions fail to match the technology investment with an investment in people. Universities currently experiencing the greatest benefits in terms of curricular improvement and market recognition are those that have staffed centers that support faculty in course redesign and development and that have provided released time, grants, credit toward tenure and promotion, and other assistance and motivation for faculty willing to engage in significant development projects. One year ago, The Pennsylvania State University's Commonwealth Educational System (CES) made an investment in limited faculty release time and instructional development support staff and laptop computers. The university acknowledged that faculty need the time, stimulation, and technical assistance to learn new strategies and incorporate them into their instruction. This initiative has produced more than 250 innovative computer-using modules that engage students in active, collaborative learning. CES campus administrators who previously saw funds spent on computers for faculty as not producing any noticeable effect now point with pride to demonstrated results.

Similarly, technology investments may fail to pay off if they are focused on inappropriate problems. Technology may often be expected to achieve outcomes it cannot produce. In particular, technology does not immediately or even inevitably reduce program delivery or computing support costs.

Another faulty assumption that can lead to unfulfilled expectations is that technology use will rapidly reduce program delivery costs—especially by means of increased student-faculty ratios or by replacing faculty with computers. The possibilities for this create anxieties for faculty. At Penn State, we find that the use of technology may improve faculty productivity, but it does not reduce the number of faculty needed. Rather, it restructures how faculty spend their time. Hours spent repetitively delivering lectures are reduced, and time spent developing new learning experiences for students and conducting extended electronic discussions with students markedly increases.

Similarly, administrators attracted to the strategy of having students bring their own computers to campus may be disappointed if they expect this to reduce computing support costs. Again, investments are redirected, but not reduced. For instance, a university may decide to have students purchase laptops. The need for computer labs may indeed be expected to diminish, but the institution may need to increase the number of "help desk" support staff, computer repair technicians, and its investment in network infrastructure.

## Where and How Is Technology Being Used to Enhance Learning?

Although it is too early to have much hard data on improved student learning or post-graduation job performance, there is a consistent pattern of enthusiastic student enrollment and of rapid institutional progress up a steep learning curve toward reliable models of instructional effectiveness.

Locations run the gamut from community colleges to graduate professional schools and from reconfigured classrooms to the home and workplace. A brief examination of some outstanding examples sheds light on the programmatic variations possible.

**Private Colleges and Universities.** Rensselaer Polytechnic Institute is a leader in studio learning ("Studio Calculus," 1994). This approach uses a single facility for instructor presentation, student work at computer workstations, and various collaborative learning activities. Studio classes are highly interactive, making it possible for each student to receive a significant amount of individual attention and individualized instruction in what have traditionally been large lecture courses. For example, the course's Web page ("Studio Calculus," 1994) described studio calculus as follows:

> Each day in Calculus students were involved in 5 basic activities: short discussions (to introduce new material or to motivate an upcoming activity and by students telling about their approach and experiences in one of the following four activities); paper and pencil activities where students work problems immediately after [the instructor] introduces new material, take time to think activities usually based on worksheets with students working in small groups to discover concepts and problem solving techniques on their own; Maple activities by small groups that allow students to discover fundamental concepts, and help students understand important ideas in calculus; and peer teaching activities whereby students in one group that have mastered one of the preceding three activities help other small groups to get the point.

Studio instruction transforms the faculty role from lecturer or presenter to coach, guide, and mentor. The instructor has fewer contact hours per course (four, as opposed to the usual seven) but more actual interaction with students. A graduate student shares the coaching role in class so that students have the advantage of at least two ways of approaching course content and activities.

Instruction is further individualized because the live and computer-based activities give the student independent control over (and responsibility for) the way in which assigned tasks are performed. As the course Web page points out, "Because they have local control of the tools, a student may explore opportunities to approach the subject matter from different directions, should the need occur. Students are encouraged to work together to solve a problem, or achieve understanding. The Studio builds socialization skills that are necessary to succeed in a team environment" ("Studio Calculus," 1994).

The studio approach is not only an attractive model for dealing with the challenge of large class enrollments. It also demonstrates how many more learning opportunities can be created while still delivering courses at one site, in a classroom, with a faculty member physically present. Studio teaching asks for a less threatening paradigm shift than does the move to asynchronous course delivery and relies less heavily on rapidly changing technologies.

Rensselaer's commitment to this and other technology-supported instructional improvements is demonstrated by its establishment of the Anderson Center for Innovation in Undergraduate Education and The International Center for Multimedia Education (ICME) ("The International Center for Multimedia Education (ICME)," 1994). Founded with the support of an impressive list of partners including AT&T, IBM, and Annenberg/The Corporation for Public Broadcasting and with significant National Science Foundation grants, the ICME is responsible not only for studio and other Rensselaer-internal projects, but for developing multimedia links with K–12 education, industry, and other institutions of higher education.

Duke's Fuqua School of Business (http://www.fuqua.duke.edu) is another outstanding example of a professional school that sees great potential payoff from a carefully orchestrated investment in computing, faculty, and curricular innovation. Like Rensselaer, Fuqua has implemented the use of technology in a way that enhances the instructor's role without totally replacing the classroom mode that is the secure "home base" of most of today's faculty. Unlike Rensselaer but like many other institutions and private organizations, Fuqua uses the technology to make a quality educational experience available to an expanded global market, and to make learning an "anytime, anywhere" experience.

In their residential, weekend, and Global Executive programs, Fuqua students use the School's Computer Mediated Learning Environment e-mail and electronic interactive bulletin board to extend discussions beyond the classroom, receive mid-project guidance from instructors, and involve more classmates in meaningful dialogue. With teamwork as an important component of their MBA programs, computers that enable working adult students to engage in asynchronous collaboration easily demonstrate their worth and contribute to delivery of meaningful learning.

In both the Fuqua and Rensselaer programs, as well as in similar programs at Carnegie-Mellon University, Drexel University, and the MIT Sloan School, it is clear that an ability to use information technology in collaborative work is one of the requirements of the professions students are preparing to enter. For these programs, justification of computer purchase requirements becomes a non-issue.

What about undergraduate liberal arts programs? Martin Ringle of Reed College, a private liberal arts institution, takes the stand that no institution claiming to educate undergraduates in a program that meets "the highest scholarly standards" can afford to bypass the outstanding curricular resources now available in a host of disciplines (Ringle, 1996).

The recent growth in the use of electronic technology across the entire undergraduate curriculum—including access to library and historic databases; simulations in the social sciences; digital imagery in art, theater, and architecture; virtual laboratories in chemistry, biology, and physics; and many other things—means that these colleges must provide their students and faculty with an appropriate level of technological tools. (Ringle, 1996).

Laurence Alvarez of the University of the South agrees, saying, "The liberal arts curriculum is designed to liberate students; to give them the basic understanding they need to maintain their education throughout their lives. . . . Colleges that do not expose their students to the proper use of technology are cheating them, and their students leave college ill equipped for the society of continual learning into which they move" (Alvarez, 1996, pp. 25–26)

**Public Universities.** Among the first initiatives of their kind, the Virtual Classroom project and its supporting Electronic Information Exchange System (EIES) were begun at the New Jersey Institute of Technology (NJIT) in 1986. As reported by Principal Investigator Starr Roxanne Hiltz (1994, pp. 243–248), a respectable amount of data have been collected and analyzed. In a project much like Penn State's Project Vision, NJIT established that the Virtual Classroom approach produced statistically significant advantages in student learning over traditional classroom instruction in mastery of course material, especially in the ability of students with differing SAT scores to achieve passing grades. Students reported satisfaction with access to educational experiences, access to their professor, course participation, and comfort using the computer. They also gave group learning experiences higher satisfaction ratings than did students not in the program.

A second generation of NJIT's EIES software incorporated word processing, database, and spreadsheet programs into the course delivery and management system. These added features produced improved student interest, effort, and satisfaction as well as improved problem-solving, decision-making, and information-synthesis skills in management simulations.

The Pennsylvania State University's Commonwealth Educational System (CES) has approached these issues from a somewhat unique vantage point. It did not start from a focus on technology acquisition or from a focus on specific upper division or graduate professional programs that obviously mandate extensive computer use. Rather, Penn State started with a strategic plan commitment to massive educational reform. In fact, the system's first focus has been on the general education courses serving the largest number of students.

Since 1994, Penn State's goal has been to transform the instructional programs at seventeen undergraduate campuses from an emphasis on teaching to an emphasis on learning (Dunham, 1993). The question then became, how do we best motivate and support large-scale change of education from a series of isolated lecture-based classroom events to an "anytime, anywhere" learning environment that is active, collaborative, and learner-responsive? Furthermore, as a state-related institution partially supported by tax dollars, Penn State was particularly sensitive to the negative possibilities inherent in requiring families to invest in computers before it had a curriculum in place that made the advantages of this purchase obvious.

Rather than start by providing or requiring students to purchase laptop computers, Penn State chose to begin retraining faculty and redesigning curricula while conducting smaller-scale projects to investigate and demonstrate the value added by offering courses that used laptops to help create a more interactive, responsive, and relevant learning environment. The CES Center for Learning and Academic Technologies (http://www.clat.psu.edu) was formed to lead and support this process.

Penn State CES's Project Vision ("Project Vision," 1995), now in its second year, enrolls a cohort of twenty entering freshmen at one of six (originally three) campuses. This program supplies students with a laptop computer and requires participation in two courses per semester redesigned to feature primarily Web-based asynchronous delivery, project-based learning; intra- and intercampus electronic team collaboration; and faculty mentoring. The courses are the same at each campus and are jointly developed by faculty with the support of instructional technologists. E-mail, First Class conferencing software, the University's library system, and the Web are the principal tools. Vision students have their own on-campus studio or "clubhouse" where they can connect to the Internet, socialize, and study together.

Challenged to move into a world without lectures, faculty studied virtual universities, asynchronous teaching and learning, and various instructional technologies. At the same time that they were charged with re-creating their courses, they were also required to work collaboratively and asynchronously with peers at distant campuses. Thus, they had to become adept at new ways of learning and working, as well as with new technologies. We are currently collecting and analyzing evaluative data. At this early stage in the game, we have observed that several important factors are at play. First, even a limited project, if it calls for massive change, can create a "big splash" effect and create significant momentum for innovation. Faculty begin to believe that the administration's commitment to reform is more than mere words. Subsequent projects have higher participation than would have been possible without this precedent.

Second, for both our faculty and our students, it is much harder to learn to collaborate effectively than it is to learn to use multimedia. Before we can begin to develop collaborative skills, most of us first need to overcome years of punishing committee project experiences. We also have to reshape attitudes and habits developed during years spent in an educational system that emphasized individual achievement. In our second year of Vision, we at Penn State are finding that both direct instruction in collaborative work and a carefully structured introduction of collaboration requirements help faculty and students adopt effective ways of working in groups.

Third, our experience has been that faculty required to make massive changes all at once will, if those changes involve technology, focus on the technology almost exclusively. The result can be technology-driven change, rather than pedagogy-driven technology utilization. One example seen frequently on course Web pages is a tendency to simply put a standard linear, print-based syllabus on the Web.

Fourth, we found that our Vision students' earned grade point averages were higher than the predicted GPAs based on their previous educational performance, even though only nine semester units of their first year's instruction were Vision classes. Students reported using skills and technologies gained in Vision when doing work for other classes.

In addition, students expressed satisfaction with the quantity and quality of instructor contact. Many mentioned that they got more personalized feedback than they did in lecture-based classes.

Faculty feedback also indicated more frequent and more comprehensive interaction with students. Faculty reported for the first time seeing, through First Class conferencing, every student's level of comprehension and skill. At first they thought students were doing more poorly. Gradually, they realized that reliance on the "stars" who participate in traditional classroom discussions may well have deceived them for years into overestimating their students' level of understanding and their own teaching effectiveness.

One important side benefit emerged at a commuter campus. One hundred percent of freshman Vision students at that campus also participated in campus organizations and activities. Our Vision experiences have shaped subsequent projects. Project Empower ("Project Empower," 1995)) has emerged as a cost-effective way to engage more faculty in technology-supported curricular innovation. With more than two hundred faculty per year now participating in this change process, we follow a number of working guidelines. We have created a structure that enables faculty to participate in multimedia course development to the extent of their interest and to have skilled assistance beyond that point. We build instructors' collaborative and multimedia skills gradually. We also encourage collaboration among natural affinity groups rather than require it among strangers.

Our approach to professional development takes advantage of the fact that faculty are adult learners. Expect a high need for ownership and control, experiential learning, and iterative learning. As researchers, faculty are particularly good at learning from mistakes. We employ significant amounts of peer modeling and teaching to encourage faculty innovation. Someone who has been a classroom teacher has far more credibility than any expert.

Finally, we use on-site instructional technologists to assist with both instructional design and technical execution. With this consultation, faculty can become familiar with the technologies and able to plan good ways to use them to foster learning. We do not expect faculty to become multimedia developers. It is more cost-effective to hire one instructional technologist to support many faculty than to pay even a handful of faculty for the time needed to develop and maintain these skills.

Our conclusion is that it is more cost-effective to engage large numbers of faculty in incremental change (say, one unit of instruction at a time) than a few faculty in extensive change. Incremental change allows iterative, experiential learning and will yield better curricular outcomes. It will also have a more pervasive impact on the total curriculum more quickly.

## Creating the New Learning Infrastructure: Who Pays?

All of the innovations just described require extensive student access to networked personal computing. Many institutions are currently struggling with the question of how to create this resource and make it accessible and affordable for all students.

A number of private and public universities are beginning to require students to bring laptop computers to school when they enter. Systems specifications help ensure that adequate, compatible equipment will be purchased. Other institutions supply the laptop, but include the cost in student fees.

A good example is Rose-Hulman Institute of Technology in Terre Haute, Indiana ("Extension of the Computer Network System," 1995). This institution, which primarily prepares students for careers in engineering, views computers and extensive campus networks as essential supports for professional education. They assert, "Innovative curricula use computing systems to reduce non-productive repetition, to facilitate understanding through graphical representation, to introduce problems that more nearly represent the real world, and to increase productivity through simulation of a wide range of engineering systems" ("Extension of the Computer Network System," 1995).

Indeed, Rose-Hulman is developing what it hopes will be a national model for project-based engineering and science education. This type of curriculum demands that significant computing power be made available to both students and faculty.

At Rose-Hulman as throughout higher education, administrators found themselves facing an expanding need for computing infrastructure investment to keep pace with the exploding volume of electronically delivered information. A decision to gradually increase the number of desktop computing facilities on campus could never keep up with demand and could impede curricular innovation. The solution they chose was to have students supply significant portions of the infrastructure.

Rose-Hulman began requiring students to bring laptops to campus starting in the fall of 1995. In addition to the curricular rationale for extensive computing resources in general, this institution concluded that

> network/power-ready laptop rooms can be prepared at a fraction of the cost of fixed-base rooms. Our estimate is that the total cost for each room is one-third the cost of the fixed-based computers.
>
> The cost of computer hardware to perform the tasks you wish will rarely decline. While the costs of units with today's capacity will decrease, the increased capacity needed for tomorrow's tasks seems to imply nearly constant cost. Our target price for the model 8086 units purchased in 1983 was the same as that for laptop computers in 1995.

> You cannot fairly compare a student's costs for the laptop solution with their costs for a fixed-base solution because laptops give computing capability outside as well as inside the classroom. A more fair approach is to compute the marginal cost for that additional capacity ["Extension of the Computer Network System," 1995].

In an effort to minimize student costs and to accommodate anticipated needs for increased computing capacity, Rose-Hulman specifies a basic machine that is easily upgradable. This is a particularly important issue with laptops. Many consumers are attracted to laptops with CD players and other features built in. However, these features rapidly become outdated and often cannot be replaced internally. A basic machine with sufficient external ports to allow attachment to the latest and greatest enhancements will have greater longevity, as well as a lower initial price.

At the University of Minnesota at Crookston (UMC), the decision was made to include the cost of the computer in student fees (Sargeant, 1995). As a state-funded institution, UMC particularly wanted to ensure that all students, regardless of income, would have equal access, and that the institution had student support for its decision. The university therefore involved both students and faculty in a extensive examination of alternatives, benefits, and costs. The end result was full student support for a quarterly $260 computer access fee that provides each student with a university-purchased (and thus standardized) laptop computer and bundled software, access to the local area network for printing and additional on-line site-licensed software. This decision was attractive to all because it provided cost savings through large group purchasing power as well as the support and learning advantages of standardizing the entire campus on one technology. The fact that this fee-based approach qualifies as a reimbursable expense for students receiving financial assistance was an essential ingredient in ensuring equal access for all students.

## Recommendations

When grappling with investments in instructional technologies, colleges and universities must consider their own unique strategic plans for market share, student access to higher education, and curricular improvement. As Richard Clark has successfully argued for over a decade, "The best current evidence is that media are mere vehicles that deliver instruction but do not influence student achievement any more than the truck that delivers our groceries causes changes in nutrition. . . . Only the content of the vehicle can influence achievement" (Clark, 1983; p. 445).

The mere presence of computers—desktop or laptop—does not intrinsically improve or make any measurable contribution to educational outcomes.

For at least the past forty years, faculty and instructional designers have been discovering how to engineer effective learning. But adequate delivery vehicles have not been available. Today's computer technologies at last have placed in our hands a vehicle capable of delivering truly learner-responsive, highly interactive, and demonstrably effective instruction. Now the challenge is to design and develop curricula that make the best use of this delivery mechanism, to fully utilize its capacities, and to integrate this technology with the human element in ways that achieve more than either the computer or the instructor could accomplish alone.

A financial commitment to instructional computing will benefit an institution to the extent that that investment is coupled with matching resource investments in people and curricula. Requiring students to purchase computers, pleading with legislators and donors for more computing dollars, and adding computer labs can backfire if these efforts produce no tangible results. It is essential that colleges and universities plan and support concomitant faculty and curricular development, so that hardware and software dollars will not be wasted.

## References

Alvarez, L. R. "Technology, Electricity and Running Water." *Educom Review*, 1996, *31* (3), 25–26.

Clark, R. E. "Reconsidering Research on Learning from Media." *Review of Educational Research*, 1983, *53* (4), 445–459.

Dunham, R. *Commonwealth Educational System Strategic Plan 1994–1997*. The Pennsylvania State University, 1993.

"Extension of the Computer Network System." Rose-Hulman Institute of Technology [http://www.fihe.org/fihe/corporate/indiana/in-roseh.htm], 1995.

Hiltz, S. R. *The Virtual Classroom: Learning Without Limits via Computer Networks*. Norwood, N.J.: Ablex, 1994.

"The International Center for Multimedia Education (ICME)." Rensselaer Polytechnic Institute [http://www.asms.rpi.edu/icme/icme.htm], 1994.

"Maricopa County Community College District Governing Board." Maricopa County Community College District [http://www.mcli.dist.maricopa.edu/mccd./vision.html], 1994.

"On Line, Learning, Interaction, and Exchange." Dallas County Community College District [http://ollie.dcccd.edu/lcedocs/main.htm], 1996.

"Project Empower." The Pennsylvania State University [http://www.clat.psu.edu/homes/projempr.htm], 1995.

"Project Vision." The Pennsylvania State University [http://www.clat.psu.edu/homes/projvis.htm], 1995.

Ringle, M. "The Well-Rounded Institution." *Educom Review*, 1996, *31* (3), 30–32.

Sargeant, D. "Mobile Computing—Reducing Time and Space Barriers." Regents of the University of Minnesota [http://www.crk.umn.edu/thinkpd.htm], 1995.

"Studio Calculus." Rensselaer Polytechnic Institute [http://ciue.rpi.edu/studio/stucalc.htm], 1994.

West, T. W. "Leveraging Technology." *Educom Review*, 1996, *31* (3), 34–35.

ANN DEDEN *is director of the Center for Learning and Academic Technologies in the Commonwealth Educational System of The Pennsylvania State University (http://www.clat.psu.edu).*

VICKI K. CARTER *is an instructional designer in the Center for Learning and Academic Technologies in the Commonwealth Educational System of The Pennsylvania State University.*

*The following chapter describes how one of the world's largest corporations taught itself to become a learning organization.*

# Enhancing Critical Thinking Skills in the Workplace

*Thomas T. Wojcik*

This chapter describes the importance of renewal *of* and *in* the workplace. It outlines key principles of renewal and their application for both the organization and the individual. The context is the corporate environment, and it is based on experiences and learning taking place at one of the world's largest pharmaceutical and chemical companies, Hoechst Celanese. The time frame is the period from 1989 to late 1996. Case studies are used to describe how the concepts of critical thinking, communication, and creative problem solving are interpreted and applied to real business situations. A large part of the experience base was developed through partnerships with other corporations and universities. The basis of this work was the Innovation Model, which was developed to provide a framework for integrating the technology, business, and human factor components needed to solve the problems associated with creating business concepts and, ultimately, commercial successes from embryonic ideas.

As organizations experience radical and accelerating change, they need to continually learn, adapt, and reorganize themselves to meet new business challenges. Because the essence of a corporation is its human and intellectual "capital," its people need to continually improve through personal growth and development. When students enter the workplace, they need to realize that their academic credentials are merely an entry ticket. This is not meant to trivialize their years of hard work in college and graduate school. It emphasizes the fact that, as educated professionals, they have entered a world of constant change, and that their academic experience taught them the fundamental principles and skills for learning, communicating, and solving problems. However, it is incumbent on each person to accept the responsibility for determining how to apply his or her academic skills and for learning how to continually learn.

The need for business renewal in the early 1990s was not self-evident in the case of Hoechst Celanese employees and therefore had to be learned. External market factors, such as the movement of much of the textile industry to factories outside of the United States, was only one example of what drove the need to change. An internal employee advertising effort was developed to heighten the awareness of individuals to the emerging crisis that would affect the careers of even those not working directly on textile fibers and related products. The extrinsic focus of the campaign was on factors such as the attrition rate of Fortune 500 companies, but the intrinsic message to employees was that they, as individuals, were subject to the same kind of obsolescence. Many, if not most, of the employees, disagreed at the time.

A fundamental premise for the development of the Innovation Model was that the learning capacity of individuals, and, subsequently, that of the organization, needed to be increased for the company to maintain its competitive advantages. We wanted first to teach ourselves, the architects of the Innovation Model, how to learn more effectively and then transfer this knowledge to others in the company. Our goal was to teach the organization how to think differently and critically and to do it in such a manner as to achieve a balanced thinking process. Dr. Edward de Bono, in his book, *Six Thinking Hats* (de Bono, 1985), describes the concept of "lateral thinking." It is a provocative mode of thinking that provides a balance with more traditional, analytical thinking. We worked toward our goal by defining and using a four-step conceptual framework beginning with developing an awareness of the need to change. Progressive steps included teaching specific skills, facilitating adoption of these lessons as natural behaviors, and, finally, institutionalizing the learning.

## Conceptual Model

We recognized the need for a conceptual model as a framework. Our approach from the beginning was very much a Research and Development (R&D) effort. We started by reading the literature and talking with experts in the field at universities, corporations, and research institutes to help with the learning process. Key contacts included Dr. Peter Senge at Massachusetts Institute of Technology about mental models and Dr. Teresa Amabile at Harvard Business School about the research basis for creative processes (Senge, 1990; Amabile, 1996; Ford and Gioia, 1995). The Innovation Model was developed based on much of this work; it consisted of three foundation elements: expertise, skills, and motivation. As a leader in the chemical industry, the *expertise* component consisted primarily of scientists and engineers and was augmented with business analysts and market researchers to produce a business team structure. The *skills* component referred to the fact that these teams would need to learn the basics of business judgment through educational programs, and the *motivation* component referred to the need to create an environment in which people would be intrinsically driven by an interest in the work itself. The fourth element, *boundary conditions,* was the distinguishing feature for the Hoechst Celanese Innovation Model, and it provided a focus for channeling the creative energy of employees. It had communication learning implications for senior management as well as the business team members. Senior management had to learn how to provide a clear description of the strategic focus for these teams, and the team members had to learn how to interpret any ambiguity in the descriptions.

The model also provided a basis for dialogue about ideas brought forward by individuals. Instead of reacting negatively to an idea that was far afield of the strategic focus, the model was used to guide discussions with employees about the challenges they would face in trying to develop a particular idea into a business concept. Those discussions first helped people to accept responsibility for championing an idea; second, they helped to build a convincing argument with a subsequent testable plan. The foundation elements, including the boundary conditions, were therefore the critical success factors for personal growth and corporate renewal (innovation). The staffing, education, environment, and strategic focus operations were the corresponding ingredients needed by the teams to achieve that growth and renewal.

Language was a key element because we had to learn to differentiate between the concepts of creativity and innovation. *Creativity* was defined as "the generation of novel and useful ideas," based on Teresa Amabile's work, and *innovation* was defined as "implementation" (Amabile, 1996). The term innovation therefore referred to a business process focused on the commercialization of ideas and business concepts. As we further developed our nomenclature by differentiating between quality and innovation—quality equating with how we do things and innovation leading to renewal—we recognized one of our first key principles. We would concentrate our initial innovation work only on discrete segments of the organization and work with employees who were both interested in and critical to successful business renewal. This contrasted with the historical approach to the quality process implementation, which was targeted at every person in the organization. Our new approach was uncomfortable because it seemed counter to the principles of the quality process. However, this turned out to be a critical success factor because it gave us a new way of dealing with both limited resources and, more importantly, the organization's limited tolerance for new initiatives.

## Office of Innovation

A mechanism was needed to test and implement the lessons learned from our research and development of the basic concepts and principles. The Office of Innovation (OoI) was created within a divisional R&D organization, the Fibers and Films Group. It initially included only two people, a senior staff director and me, as the business manager. It was set up with two key operating principles.

The first was that we would not judge peoples' ideas, and the second was that we would not do the work to develop their ideas. Personal accountability and responsibility were targeted as primary expectations of the learning process. These principles were articulated and explained to employees, who subsequently reacted, not surprisingly, with skepticism and cynicism. Once again, the usage of an operating principle helped us and the organization to learn the importance of accepting personal responsibility for developing an idea into something concrete. It helped people to understand that they needed not only to generate novel ideas, but that these ideas needed to be useful, and that *they* needed to be responsible for doing the work to develop the ideas. Everyone quickly learned that the traditional employee suggestion box system was ineffective because it involved no accountability and therefore yielded only limited benefits.

The primary job of the OoI was to help employees find high-quality ideas: those that are truly novel and useful and that would therefore have a high probability of delivering a significant value-added benefit to the company. Since the infrastructure of the corporation was set up for large-volume, highly capital-intensive manufacturing, employees needed to learn the magnitude and type of ideas that would most aptly fit this system. The OoI operated as an "influential assist" to help individuals understand and interpret senior management directives such as "to work only on projects which had the potential for generating $5–10 million in earnings in 3–5 years." Senior management also had to learn through constant dialogue with the scientists and business analysts how to effectively communicate their vision and direction in achieving the financial goals by helping employees understand what kinds of ideas were appropriate.

A large-scale example of an experiment for these purposes was the design and construction of an Innovation Laboratory. The idea came from a need to find a better place to house a computer brainstorming system that had been purchased from Virginia PolyTechnic Institute and State University. Initially, the plan consisted of preparing a standard engineering approval request. But, when we started to assemble a team of designers, we stopped and reminded ourselves to "practice what we were preaching." We then recruited a team of approximately thirty people from inside and outside the company. These included the obvious—company draftsmen and engineers—and the unusual—outside artists, writers, architects, furniture suppliers, electrical contractors, and others. The team produced a very unusual design with a price tag of $310,000 (in 1991) for the five-hundred-square-foot facility. Everyone on the team felt that this figure was high, and more importantly, nobody would volunteer to present the proposed budget to senior management. The team then went through a series of reevaluation and creative problem-solving exercises, developed some unique options, and agreed (albeit somewhat grudgingly) to an arbitrary budget of $75,000 (VanGundy, 1988). (That figure equated to the typical cost of remodeling a standard conference room on-site at the time.) The lab was built within that new budget figure, but more importantly, by thinking and being extremely resourceful, the team actually produced a very creative product, the Innovation Lab. It became a focal point for team learning and a symbol of the importance of different thinking styles.

## Education

Education is the classical route to personal renewal and growth. Team learning is a current, popular name for a means by which people can collectively grow and continually learn together. Concepts like organizational learning and systems thinking have been well researched and documented by numerous experts, but it has been difficult to apply these concepts to actual business situations (Senge, 1990). We recognized this problem and sought to develop a more formalized teaching process. The objective was to teach ourselves how to learn to better interact with each other and in particular, how scientists and engineers could better interact with business, marketing, and sales professionals. The cyclical adult learning model of planning, doing, reflecting was the conceptual framework used to guide the course development. Once again, we put our principles into action and used an R&D approach. We read the literature, worked with experts in the field of organizational learning and creative problem solving, and then constructed an experiment called *IT101*, an acronym for the Innovation Training 101 course.

IT101 was conceived and structured as an experiential learning process. The objective was to teach students—our employees—the fundamental principles of business judgment in an environment where they could simultaneously practice application of the lessons learned. It was in essence a two-week course conducted during a three-month time frame in a number of different "classrooms." Only teams, not individuals, participated, and the admission requirement was that each team needed to bring a real, rudimentary idea that could be developed into a business concept proposal by the end of the course. The teaching staff was recruited from experts in the fields of behavioral psychology, venture capital management, strategic business planning, creative education, and athletic training. Parts of IT101 were taught in traditional classrooms while others were conducted in remote outdoor locations where the students were not distracted by telephones, e-mail, and other interruptions.

The IT101 experiment was a success from a number of perspectives. First, the students did indeed learn how to transform an idea into a business concept proposal as evidenced by the final exam results: the successful presentation of their proposals to a board of venture capitalists. Second, everyone (the organization) learned about a broader definition of business success. Third, the organization learned a better way of learning. This is not to say that IT101 in and of itself was the better way. It was, however, representative of a means by which an organization can craft new ways of learning by continuing to develop and experiment with different models of teaching.

As the lessons from the IT101 experiment were being digested by and integrated into the organization, the Office of Innovation's role was expanded from the divisional to the corporate R&D level. Coincident with this change,

Dr. R. G. Cooper's Stage/Gate model (Cooper, 1993) was being refined and adapted as the commercialization process of choice for new businesses in Hoechst Celanese. Subsequently, the education process had to be transformed, and the concept of externalization became the next principle to be learned and practiced by the organization.

## Externalization

*Externalization* is the process for examining yourself and your organization by working closely with such outsiders as customers, competitors, suppliers, universities, government labs, and others to get a better understanding of your own organization.

The traditional approach for industrial scientists and engineers was to work on projects that had been assigned by a senior manager. Objectives, deadlines, and performance criteria were clearly spelled out for the employee. Although this was more straightforward, if not necessarily easier, for the employees, the approach had inherent problems. Most notable was that there were no independent criteria for continually testing the validity of a particular concept against performance standards for business value. Sponsorship by a senior manager was a critical factor, and this was highly dependent on the personal commitment, or championship, of that person rather than on a set of strategic imperatives and milestones. The changing business environment of the 1990s required the use of another, more objective approach. Management became acutely aware of this necessity because of competitive business pressures. Experienced employees as well as new hires from universities realized they had to develop new skills and learn how to find and justify new project ideas. In other words, they had to learn how to write a business plan before beginning to work on their projects. They would have to learn how to apply their lessons learned from universities and workshops such as IT101.

Critical thinking took on a new dimension in that people now had to learn how to apply the fundamentals of business planning and team operation. They would work closely with a prospective customer, for example, to attempt to identify an unmet market need that would benefit from a technology or product that could be developed within the strategic focus (the boundaries) of the company. Team leaders and managers experienced in marketing and customer technical service activities would mentor and teach the team members how to ferret out information from meetings with prospective customers, but the need became clear for more rigorous training. We looked outside for assistance, and found a small, entrepreneurial company—SIMCO, Inc.—that specializes in market-focused product development. Their search and appraise process was subsequently adapted to the Hoechst Celanese situation whereby team members were taught the true meaning of the Pareto principle of diminishing returns and how to apply it. For example, instead of the teams investing a lot of time and money to develop a robust technology demonstration, they learned how to produce "concept prototypes" after having interactive discussions with a customer. The search and appraise workshop, like IT101, was an experience-based situation in which employees learned how to communicate with a prospective customer to determine their true needs. In fact, the experience had a number of learning levels, the first of which was to discuss and identify the unmet need. The next level involved learning to differentiate between what was needed and what was merely wanted. Ultimately, the teams were taught to communicate in a manner such that they and the prospective customer would simultaneously identify an unmet need that the customer did not yet know about. Therefore, the communication and thinking processes were elevated to the point where both were learning together.

At this point, it is useful and important to think about the evolution of this learning process. IT101 was an experience-based teaching situation in which employees learned the basics of business judgment and business plan composition. Search and appraise was an interactive teaching situation in which the Hoechst Celanese team members and a prospective customer would together learn about an unmet need, which may not have been known previously by either party. As people practiced and applied these lessons, they found that another dimension, relationship building, was becoming the next critical success factor.

The experiential workshop approach was again used as a key teaching component to help employees to deal with the subtleties and nuances of customer relationship operations. However, the principle behind the approach to IT101 was once again applied to this situation. First, teachers from market research firms were hired and asked to teach us how they work with customers *and* how they teach their employees to grow in this area. We subsequently created "Voice of the Customer" workshops for our own employees to learn from those experiences. Second, a technique termed "Customer Days" was developed, whereby large groups of Hoechst Celanese employees would participate in a series of two-day seminars with senior technical and business people from a key, existing customer. The obvious technical learning and sharing would occur during the presentations and formal meeting parts of the agenda, but, in addition, people experienced relationship-building lessons during the informal dinner, breakfast, and lunch meetings as well as during small-group, intercompany brainstorm sessions. The third, and possibly most effective, technique was to arrange visits and meetings at specific customer facilities and to coach and mentor employees in working with these external partners. Once again, some of the key learning occurred outside of the normal teaching environment: for example, while at airport gates waiting to return home after the meeting. Active listening was a major communications learning requirement, and it often proved the most difficult for people to master.

As we worked to enrich these customer relationships, we recognized the benefits of creating a more sophisticated process, which we termed the "Customer-Pull Partnership" (CPP). The technical organization was already structured as market and product application-oriented focus teams as a result of the business-driven strategy development during recent years. The distinguishing feature of the CPP is that it targets specific companies as compared to industries and markets. Once again, this concept arose from our constant critical thinking and problem-solving process. In essence, we had reframed the entire concept of business-driven technology development and consequently identified an important, albeit subtly distinct, avenue to finding unmet market needs.

## Conclusion

Much time and money was invested in teaching people how to think and approach problems differently, and many companies have done this in the 1990s. The primary difficulty is getting people to internalize teachings to help the organization proceed along the learning pathway. Team learning situations included individually focused topics, but these were eventually related back to the team situation. For example, the Myers-Briggs Type Indicator (MBTI) was used to help people understand their own personality styles and how these affected their relationships with others on the team. Use of MBTI is fairly widespread in corporations, and it is being used in many university curricula to prepare students for the concept of personality typing on the job. We found it to be quite useful as people readily adopted the concept and applied it to their job situations. The real lesson is that everyone is responsible for thinking critically about what they are apparently being taught on a particular subject, talking about it through substantive communication with others, and then defining and solving the problem of applying it to their situation.

MBTI helped individuals to understand and work with others having different personality styles. Another approach to facilitating the self-awareness learning process about critical thinking skill development is the 360-degree feedback instrument. Briefly stated, this is a process by which an individual works with a behavioral psychologist, who gathers data about the individual through a series of confidential, anonymous interviews with others in the organization. I participated in the process and received much useful feedback about how to improve my own performance and problem-solving abilities in the company. More important, however, I extended my own learning process by working closely with the psychologist to develop a deeper understanding of the human factors affecting business renewal in the organization. This subsequently helped to expand the innovation model to include behavioral psychological factors in addition to the business skills and technology components of corporate renewal. Our "more-educated" view therefore integrated human behavior, technology, and project management disciplines with creativity, innovation, and commercialization process functions to form a more comprehensive model of renewal.

The ultimate challenge is not in teaching people creative thinking tools and techniques. There are unlimited courses, workshops, and seminars available through universities and consulting firms to accomplish that objective (Racz and Wojcik, 1994). The true challenge is in teaching people how to apply their lessons, and that is where we focused most of our intellectual energy during the past several years. Corporations exist to produce profits for the stockholders, and the employees need to learn how to keep their intellectual energy focused to that end. The operative word is *learn*, and it requires a continuing search for a better, personal understanding of the thinking process. We are constantly searching for better ways of applying principles and theories we learn to the task at hand. We created a number of experimental university partnerships to determine how to do managed discovery research to augment our internal R&D efforts. In addition to learning new technologies, we are learning different ways of doing research and development and business analysis from these relationships. The universities are also learning how to interface and work more efficiently and effectively with the corporate world.

The real paradigm shift for corporations (and universities) is that their employees (students) are no longer expected only to successfully complete projects assigned *to them*. They are expected to determine which ideas are of interest to the organization, develop a convincing argument for a specific project idea, structure it as a business concept proposal, get it approved, and successfully complete the project development and business plan.

This paradigm shift is itself an opportunity for experimenting with different approaches of evaluating and solving problems. It is driven by the profit motive of corporations, but it will ultimately succeed only if individuals take the initiative to learn and to try different approaches for thinking, communicating, and solving problems creatively. Their curiosity and intrinsic motivation to learn will change not only how people work, but it will make the work environment a true learning organization.

## References

Amabile, T. *Creativity in Context.* Boulder, Colo.: Westview Press, 1996.

Cooper, R. G. *Winning at New Products; Accelerating the Process from Idea to Launch.* (2nd ed.) New York: Addison-Wesley, 1993.

de Bono, E. *Six Thinking Hats.* New York: Little, Brown, 1985.

Ford, C. M., and Gioia, D. A. *Creative Action in Organizations; Ivory Tower Visions and Real World Voices.* Thousand Oaks, Calif.: Sage, 1995.

Racz, R., and Wojcik, T. T. *The Creativity Handbook; Tools for Creative Business and Personal Problem-Solving.* Buffalo, N.Y.: Creative Education Foundation, 1994.

Senge, P. M. *The Fifth Discipline: The Art and Practice of the Learning Organization.* New York: Doubleday, 1990.

VanGundy, A. B. *Techniques of Structured Problem Solving.* (2nd ed.) New York: Van Nostrand Reinhold, 1988.

THOMAS T. WOJCIK *is the manager of Hoechst Celanese Corporation's Office of Innovation in Charlotte, N.C.*

*When educators make public their expectations for student learning and use those expectations to navigate their teaching, students are better prepared for life in and beyond the classroom.*

# Improving Teaching and Learning Effectiveness by Defining Expectations

*Carole E. Barrowman*

A few years ago, I conducted a workshop for the faculty of a liberal arts college in the South. I had spent most of the morning session discussing assessment, exploring the relationship between teaching and learning, and stressing the importance of using criteria to give direction to students for learning. My audience was glazing over. We all needed a break.

As the faculty regrouped, the young man who had been videotaping the workshop waved his hands madly at the back of the auditorium. He was a work-study student at the college. These were his teachers. I asked him if he had something he wanted to say. He did.

Addressing the entire auditorium, he proclaimed, "If I had known what I was supposed to learn, I might not have failed so many classes."

Almost twenty years ago in her seminal work, *Errors and Expectations: A Guide for the Teacher of Basic Writing* (1977, p. 275), Mina Shaughnessy had this student in mind when she explored how "the expectations of learners and teachers powerfully influence what happens in schools." To Shaughnessy this was "both reassuring and disturbing," reassuring because students might rise above our expectations, but "disturbing" because students might just as frequently let low expectations become self-fulfilling prophesies (1977, p. 275). Shaughnessy's philosophy and pedagogical concerns about expectations have reached beyond conversations about the teaching of writing to find colleagues from a variety of disciplines in national discussions about teaching and learning in general.

Organizations such as the American Association for Higher Education (AAHE) and the Association of American Colleges and Universities are adding their voices to this growing discourse. A recent publication by The Teaching

Initiative for AAHE, *Making Teaching Community Property: A Menu for Peer Collaboration and Peer Review,* edited by Pat Hutchings (1996), is a compilation of just such dialogues. Written by faculty from diverse institutions investigating issues of teaching, learning, and assessment, two distinctive pedagogical patterns seem to be emerging from these conversations.

Firstly, when the pedagogy in our classroom changes from one of seeing ourselves as teachers of subject areas to seeing ourselves as teachers of students, the result is a profound change in the way we define ourselves as professionals and scholars. Faculty welcoming this reconceptualization value teaching as "scholarly work," demanding a more sophisticated "process of ongoing inquiry and reflection," about the complexities of teaching than our profession has afforded it in the past (Hutchings, 1996, p. 1). Teaching is no longer just about "standing and delivering" (p. 1), but instead is about facilitating students to become "authentic participants" in the classroom (p. 106).

Teaching as a scholarly practice demands a systematic reconceptualization of not just our classroom practice and our curricula, but our particular identities as educators. Teaching must become a scholarly pursuit that involves rethinking the nature of disciplinary expertise (Schulman, 1993). Tim Riordan (1993, p.2) argues from a similar perspective that this revision of teaching as "substantive scholarship" means "we must study our students as well as our disciplines," and that we take "active measures to elicit from and be attentive to the ways in which our own students learn most effectively."

The second pattern emerging in this national conversation is a direct result of the first and a focus of this chapter. Viewing teaching as a valued mode of scholarly inquiry means that we have to become more accountable for its results—student learning. When, as educators, we make public our expectations for student learning, and we use those expectations to navigate our teaching, our students are better prepared for life in and beyond the classroom.

## Institutional Perspective

For over twenty-five years, the faculty at Alverno College in Milwaukee, Wisconsin, have been teaching in ways that reflect these two distinctive emerging patterns. As a liberal arts college with an urban population of approximately twenty-three hundred students, Alverno College has created a culture in which faculty facilitate student learning in eight ability areas, using the disciplines as contexts in which students demonstrate their intellectual development. Alverno's system of assessment-as-learning puts students at the center of a dynamic learning process that connects their education to their future lives and work. Analysis, problem solving, and communication are three of the essential abilities at the core of Alverno's curriculum, along with valuing in a decision-making context, effective citizenship, taking global perspectives, social interaction, and aesthetic responsiveness. Alverno students demonstrate these abilities in increasingly complex ways as they work through the college's general education program and into their chosen major areas.

However, these eight abilities are more than a set of discrete skills. They are a complex set of integrated, developmental, and transferable abilities whose definitions are the result of ongoing conversations with faculty, students, alumni, and present and future employers of Alverno students (Mentkowski, 1991, pp. 10–13). We have discovered that when students are taught complex multidimensional abilities like critical thinking and effective communication, student learning not only transfers into other disciplines during their college work, but the practice of these abilities transfers into the student's performances in the work place (Mentkowski and Rogers, 1993, p. 35).

This understanding about the transference of learning comes from years of practice studying what constitutes effective teaching and its outcome—student learning. By defining ourselves as teacher-scholars, we, as faculty, spend a considerable amount of professional time fine-tuning what it means to teach well. Alverno's culture accommodates these ongoing conversations in a number of ways. Let me share two.

At three formal times during the year, faculty gather as a corporate group for extensive workshops and presentations on issues that have grown out of our teaching at that particular time. We share teaching philosophies and pedagogy and classroom successes and failures, and in recent years we have listened to a series of panel discussions in which current Alverno students and recent graduates have shared their experiences as learners in Alverno's culture. These Alverno Institutes, for which faculty share in planning and production, are integral to the intellectual life of the college. Through this institute structure, faculty and administrators also developed, drafted, and revised Alverno's criteria for effective teaching, which are part of the process for faculty promotion in rank.

Lee Schulman (1993, p. 6) advocates faculty's coming together to discuss teaching around the traditional disciplines, because they are "the basis for our intellectual communities." The disciplines can be a good place to start. However, as a catalyst for collaboration they can quickly become constricting. Too rarely do faculty address significant teaching issues as part of their disciplinary discourse. Also, for many faculty, too often the seeds of our discontent, either as teachers or researchers, are rooted in our disciplines. Sooner or later, we need to come together using our students as the basis of our "intellectual communities."

At Alverno, another way we allow for conversations about teaching and learning is through interdisciplinary department groupings in which the eight abilities students are developing are the basis of the collaborative community. No classes are scheduled on Friday afternoons, to free up time for these groupings to meet regularly during a semester. For example, I am a member of the English department, but I'm also chair of the communication ability department. Membership in the communication department comes from a variety of disciplines, including nursing, mathematics, and the sciences. The communication department's charge is to maintain the quality and effectiveness of the teaching, learning, and assessment of speaking, writing, reading, listening, and visual, computer, and quantitative literacies across Alverno's curriculum (Alverno College Faculty, 1984). Underpinning the communication department's work is the assumption that students, by the time they graduate, are effective communicators in their discipline and in their varied social contexts. The ability-based departments share in the curricular decision-making processes of the institution and contribute to the college's overall scholarship of teaching. An explicit assumption of this kind of institutional structure is that a curriculum is something organic that can benefit from regular scrutiny from varied perspectives as to how well it is graduating successful students.

At the heart of what we do at Alverno is the organizing principle that student abilities articulated in public criteria shape the pedagogy in our courses and programs. This principle results in student learning that can be measured through assessment and self-assessment. Students develop essential abilities like communication and analysis most successfully when they know exactly what they are setting out to learn; when, as educators, we let those expectations shape our assessment of that learning; and when we develop curricular coherence in our classrooms and our programs based on those public expectations. Students who learn in a coherent system transfer their learning from course to course and eventually into the workplace more successfully (Loacker, 1991).

A great deal has been written in other places detailing Alverno's broader theory of assessment-as-learning (Alverno College Faculty, 1984; Loacker and Mentkowski, 1993). For the purpose of this volume's themes and this particular chapter's focus, the following questions are the most relevant. How do we define expectations for student learning? How do these expectations reshape our teaching and learning and bring coherence to a curriculum?

Alverno faculty's experience with ability-based teaching and learning can offer significant principles to higher education as we all seek new ways to structure our classrooms and meet the teaching and learning demands of a new century of students.

## Defining Expectations to Shape Teaching and Learning

Faculty expectations for student learning should be defined at a more specific level the closer those expectations are to the student's actual classroom performance. At the institutional level the most general expectation is, in a sense, a college or university's mission statement. At Alverno, our eight abilities grew out of the spirit of our mission statement and the needs of our students when they graduated. Institutional outcomes are by nature general and largely decontextualized. One of the problems for many faculty struggling to hold themselves and their students more accountable for student learning is that the faculty's expectations for students are often never clearly defined beyond the institutional level.

If the goal of clarifying expectations is to help students learn from those expectations and independently transfer the processes and knowledge inherent in the expectations to future learning and work, to leave our expectations vague and only generally defined is not effective teaching. Alverno's faculty use a continuum of increasing specificity as a means of clarifying and defining our outcomes for students (Alverno College Faculty, 1994, pp. 28, 36–37).

In this continuum, each program or discipline department takes the college's institutional outcomes and integrates them into the context of their students' learning needs, increasing the level of specificity of the outcome and contextualizing it in disciplinary content. A program outcome is the integration of knowledge and dispositions, of ideas and processes (Alverno College Faculty, 1994, p. 8). As an outcome travels along this continuum of increasing specificity, journeying closer to a student's actual performance, the outcome becomes full and rich with disciplinary ideas and processes that can shape student learning. A student outcome at the program level is both a navigator's compass providing direction for that learning and a mathematician's two-pronged compass reflecting the rippling patterns of a student's developing knowledge and abilities.

## Disciplinary Perspective

Wayne Booth (1965, p. 202) advocated creating disciplinary programs of study that "think about the skills that are really needed by a student." He also argued that English teachers should recognize that "there is no necessary connection . . . between the shaping of catalogues and the shaping of minds" (p. 201). About the issue of content in English, Booth believed that coverage "is not in the least what we have in mind when we think of competence or distinction in our field" (p. 202).

The following examples of student outcomes at the program level are two of six that Alverno's English department expects students majoring in the discipline to be able to demonstrate when they have completed our program of study. These expectations represent contextualizing, through a disciplinary lens, the institution's general student outcomes of analysis and communication. They also represent what we think Booth meant when he asked the profession to teach for "distinction in our field":

1. To use frameworks to analyze, evaluate, and place in context literary works from various cultures and genres.
2. To communicate an understanding of literary criticism and question its assumptions.

These student expectations at the program level provide direction for learning in Alverno's English courses. In the first two courses of our sequence, we cannot expect our students to meet the above outcomes. The students are, after all, just beginning. Fourth- or fifth-semester students need to master a few intellectual steps in the critical thinking process first, and they also must work with the content of English. The need for increasing the specificity of our outcomes is critical, though. Our expectations should become more qualitative and descriptive as they move closer to the student in action in our classroom. At the same time, outcomes must characterize the developmental level of that student.

The more specific expectations, then, that shape the first course (English 210) in the English sequence are

1. To develop the ability to do close reading as a method of analyzing and responding to literature.
2. To recognize several major critical approaches: their nature, assumptions, usefulness, and relation to close analytical reading.

Note the increased detail in these expectations and how they have now become contextualized in some of the content and processes of an effective English major: the ability to read closely, critically, and with a mastery of some literary criticism. These outcomes are the course goals, which are made public to students in the syllabus and referred to throughout the class when working on a project or activity that demonstrates some learning in relation to them. Like our assumptions about a curriculum, we, as Alverno faculty, use our syllabi as contracts with the students for their learning.

As the course instructor, my job is not just to lecture on the various schools of literary criticism or to share a few critical insights on the various novels read in relation to that criticism. Instead, my challenge is to create the kind of classroom learning environment that allows students to become literary critics. Therefore, I do most of my work outside of the class, developing structures and strategies, preparing materials and assessments, and giving meaningful feedback so that students can do most of their work inside the classroom. Students are ultimately responsible for their own learning. I am responsible for making it possible.

At Alverno, we try to create assessments that bring the student as close as possible to a situation in which she will be using her learning in life beyond the classroom (Alverno College Faculty, 1994, p. 19). A few years ago, a published report (Lloyd-Jones and Lundsford, 1989, pp. 25–26) from the College Strand of The English Coalition Conference, "Democracy Through Language," expressed this same desire, that "English studies be based on practices," and that English courses be organized around "critical inquiry, collaboration, and conscious theorizing." The explication of the following in-course assessment, presently used in a beginning Alverno English course, demonstrates the above pedagogical patterns.

Two Wisconsin school districts have earned the dubious distinction of regularly attempting to ban library books. Alverno's English department designed the following assessment to connect with this routine occurrence. (Many departments at Alverno team-design courses, although we rarely team teach.) The most specific generation of the English course's outcomes is visible in both the criteria used to judge the students' performance and the criteria the peer assessors and the students themselves use. To be successful in this assessment (Alverno College English Department, 1994) students need to have carefully read and explored Toni Morrison's *Sula.*

### EN 310: PRACTICING LITERARY CRITICISM

**Assessment Three**

In a small-group setting, you are to take on the role of a member of the Milwaukee school district's curriculum council. The council has been asked to review Toni Morrison's novel *Sula,* that is being taught to a senior college prep class. Some members of the local PTA consider the book, "detrimental to the moral development of their children." At the conclusion of today's meeting, you will have to make a decision about whether or not the novel should be retained for classroom use. You will then have to be prepared to face the PTA and explain your decision. [The instructor provides a series of questions to aid this discussion.]

**Selected Criteria**

(The following criteria are used to assess the student's performance.)

For Student Peer Review:
1. Describe how and where the student integrated her learning of the concepts of literary criticism into her arguments.
2. What should this student do to improve her analysis? Give specific suggestions based on your observations today.

For Instructor Use:
1. Student identifies possible objections to the teaching of *Sula* to a senior college prep class and identifies possible arguments for keeping *Sula* in the curriculum.
2. Student accurately summarizes arguments and identifies values underlying the arguments of both sides of the issue.
3. Throughout the decision-making process, the student makes specific references to the novel itself, noting relevant aspects of plot, character etc.
4. Student makes specific references to three critical perspectives, connecting them to the task at hand.

At the most particular level of the continuum of increasing specificity, the course outcomes have become assessment criteria used to judge a student's performance. I use the criteria when I write feedback to the student evaluating her performance. The best way for an instructor to measure a student's capacity to perform a particular ability or aspect of that ability is to look at the corresponding behavior (Alverno College Faculty, 1994, p. 19).

This particular English assessment demands that students practice a level of critical thinking, including the ability to summarize, synthesize, draw relationships among differing ideas, and take a position from those ideas that will serve them well in any workplace. Students also leave this course with an appreciation for good literature and the critical theories that have grown from it.

For criteria to be effective tools for shaping and defining student learning, they need to be an integration of the knowledge and the abilities necessary in the performance. Criteria need to be open-ended enough to elicit excellence and broad enough in their specificity to define a variety of possible student responses (Alverno College Faculty, 1994, p. 33). One of my many mistakes as a developing teacher using criteria was writing them in such a way that they suggested only one possible performance—mine.

Like Luther, we all have our lists of indulgences, the things we will tolerate or not tolerate in work submitted to us, such as requiring that no ragged notebook paper be used and that everything be double spaced. These are not criteria. Using format requirements and directions as criteria often results in performances that lack depth or critical definition. Criteria should create a picture of an ability. Directions, like length requirements and typing requirements, are, in a sense, pre-criteria. They may need to be met before evaluating a student's work (Alverno College Faculty, 1994, p. 114).

It is important to note that structuring the learning in a course following a continuum of increasing specificity from the institutional level into the student's performance is not always a linear, top-down process. Sometimes I may create the idea for an assignment and design from that point. At other times, I might recognize a need in my students, define my performance criteria first, and then create the assignment. The key, however, is to let the expectations for what students should know and do with their learning shape the teaching, no matter the level of specificity at which one begins. Expectations that remain in the hall when class begins or are printed only in the syllabus and not discussed after the first day are meaningless.

## Defining Expectations for Coherence Across a Curriculum

Defining expectations with an increasing level of specificity from the institutional level to the program level and into the classroom results in curricular coherence. Alverno faculty have found that this kind of coherence enhances students' abilities to transfer their learning from one course to another. Defining expectations at an institutional level also can raise the general quality of student performance across a curriculum. Alverno's college-wide criteria for effective communication constitute an example of such a set of expectations that shape teaching and learning and provide coherence in the curriculum.

For decades colleges and universities have expected students to be able to communicate effectively when they graduate. Many faculty, though, still privilege only writing in this expectation. As citizens of an increasingly technological culture, simply preparing students to be able to write effectively as their predominant mode of communication is not effective teaching. According to

Alverno's Communication Ability Department, students who can communicate effectively habitually make meaning by connecting with everything involved in communication: people, ideas, texts, media, and technology. They integrate a variety of communication abilities (speaking, writing, listening, reading, quantitative, and media literacy) to meet the demands of increasingly complex communication situations.

This description of an effective communicator, though detailed, is still quite generic. However, the discussion of the following in-class history assessment, currently used at Alverno in a third-semester history course, demonstrates how one teacher uses this generic outcome for integrated communication as the framework by which he teaches a historical period.

### HS 308: Topics in United States History to the Civil War

#### Assessment 2

As Americans engaged in colonial resistance, revolution and the creation of a new nation, their perceptions of themselves and their views of society were altered. These revolutionary experiences compelled many Americans to clarify their political beliefs, values and their vision of what kind of society they wanted to live in.

Your local library is offering a series of lectures on the revolutionary experience as part of the town's Fourth of July celebration. In an attempt to make the period more meaningful to a modern audience, the library board wants to focus the series around the personal perspectives of a variety of participants in the American Revolution.

You have been asked to give a presentation from one of the perspectives listed below. Prepare a speech in which you explain how the events of the American Revolution and the creation of a new nation affected you. Describe how your experiences altered your perception of yourself, your roles in society, your relationship with others and your hopes for the future of the new nation. Be sure to include specific experiences to illustrate the changes you describe [Casey, 1995].

The student is asked to choose from a list of perspectives, including a Virginia planter, an artisan from Boston, a female friend of Abigail Adams, a poor North Carolina farmer who fought supporting the revolution, a farm woman and mother, an African slave of a revolutionary planter, a wealthy New York merchant, and a Native American from a tribe affected by the Revolution. The instructor creates research packets consisting of primary documents, readings, and illustrations that correspond with each perspective and organizes at least three weeks of his course around this assessment.

Students first explore the materials independently, summarizing and synthesizing their conclusions. They then come together in like groups of planters, farm women, and so on, and they make choices about what conclusions and events are most critical from their reading and research. Before the students formally present, they work in mixed groups, pretending to be a farmer, a slave, an artisan, and so on, debating what issues and ideas had the most impact on their particular person's perspective. The instructor guides these discussions with questioning prompts.

The students in this class are made aware of the coherence that shapes the choices their teacher has made in a couple of critical ways. As this assessment is presented to them, the instructor makes explicit how their work during this project will provide evidence for their demonstrating the following course goals: to make explicit connections between individual pieces of historical information, to communicate empathy with diverse historical perspectives, and to communicate a sensitivity to gender and cultural issues as they relate to historical study.

## Selected Assessment Criteria

The following specific criteria by which this faculty member judges the students' performances are included with the assignment when he distributes it to them.

1. Accurately explained how the beliefs, values, and ideals of the person whose perspective you spoke from were shaped by his or her revolutionary experiences.
2. Accurately showed how your personal history is based on a clear understanding of assigned readings, class discussions, and presentations.
3. Your presentation was given without reliance on scripted or memorized input and throughout your presentation you showed how your ideas and their sources contributed to your thinking.

This assessment is an integrated communication performance in history. With this presentation and the processes leading up to it, these history students personify Alverno's generic outcome for effective communication. In the planning and researching for a presentation, the student has read historical data, listened to the ideas and conclusions of others, drafted his or her own ideas and conclusions, and, finally, pulled it all together into an engaging and organized presentation. Through this assessment and the class time given to preparing for it, the student has become a historian, making meaning about the past and independently interpreting its events. The student has learned history by managing a complex communication situation.

The fact that the instructor holds students accountable for not only their learning in history, but also their communication abilities, further reinforces curricular coherence for the students. The speaking and writing criteria by which this instructor assesses students are printed on card stock and attached to the syllabus of his course. These discrete communication criteria are faculty-generated and used by all faculty across the curriculum. By teaching and reinforcing common expected levels of communication as a complex integrated ability, Alverno faculty teach in such a way that a balance of the modes is developed consistently in their classrooms. This use of criteria also redistributes the weight of teaching communication from the backs of only the departments of speech and English to the shoulders of all faculty and students.

## Conclusions

In a curriculum giving students a clear sense of what and why they are learning, teaching becomes much more an art of improvisation and imagination than it may be when lecturing is the dominant mode. When outcomes shape teaching, instructors ask different questions as they plan courses. "What will I cover?" becomes "What do I want students to know and be able to do at the end of this class? Beyond the class?" The latter questions shift the emphasis in choosing course materials from teacher preferences to student needs. When "we identify an ability as an outcome, we have the beginning statement of what we are assessing" (Alverno College Faculty, 1994, p. 29) and what we need to teach.

Effective teaching is more than developing a bag of tricks and "cannot be equated with [just] technique. . . . Faculty and administrators who encourage talk about teaching despite its vagaries are treasures among us" (Palmer, 1990, p. 11–12). Parker Palmer believes that "more engaging ways of teaching will take root only as we explore more engaged images of knowing."

When assumptions and philosophies of teaching and learning are regularly discussed in institutions of higher learning, when teaching practice is valued as a critical part of the profession, and when learning expectations are shared with students and colleagues the result can be an energetic culture of learning: a culture in which successes and challenges call out from open classroom doors and are heard by all of us.

## References

Alverno College English Department. "English 210 Course Assessment." Milwaukee, Wis.: Alverno College Institute, 1994.

Alverno College Faculty. *Student Assessment-as-Learning at Alverno College.* Milwaukee, Wis.: Alverno College Institute, 1994.

Alverno College Faculty. *Analysis and Communication at Alverno: An Approach to Critical Thinking.* Milwaukee, Wis.: Alverno Productions, 1984.

Booth, W. "The Undergraduate Program." In J. C. Gerber (ed.), *The College Teaching of English.* New York: Appleton-Century-Crofts, 1965.

Casey, K. "History 308 Course Assessment." Milwaukee, Wis.: Alverno College History Department, 1995.

Hutchings, P. (ed.). *Making Teaching Community Property: A Menu for Peer Collaboration and Peer Review.* Washington, D.C.: American Association for Higher Education, 1996.

Lloyd-Jones, R., and Lundsford, A. (eds.). "Report of the College Strand." In *The English Coalition Conference: Democracy Through Language.* Urbana, Ill.: National Council of Teachers of English, 1989.

Loacker, G. "Designing a National Assessment System: Alverno's Institutional Perspective." Paper commissioned by U.S. Department of Education, National Center for Educational Statistics, 1991.

Loacker, G., and Mentkowski, M. "Creating a Culture Where Assessment Improves Learning." In T. W. Banta and Associates (eds.), *Making a Difference: Outcomes of a Decade of Assessment in Higher Education.* San Francisco: Jossey-Bass, 1993.

Mentkowski, M. *Designing a National Assessment System: Assessing Abilities That Connect Education and Work.* Paper commissioned by U.S. Department of Education, National Center for Education Statistics, 1991.

Mentkowski, M., and Rogers, G. "Connecting Education, Work, and Citizenship: How Assessment Can Help." *Metropolitan Universities: An International Forum,* 1993, 4 (1), 34–36.

Palmer, P. J. "Good Teaching: A Matter of Living the Mystery." *Change,* Jan./Feb. 1990, pp. 10–16.

Riordan, T. *Nature of Teaching.* Milwaukee, Wis.: Alverno College Institute, 1993.

Schulman, S. L. "Teaching as Community Property: Putting an End to Pedagogical Solitude." *Change,* Nov./Dec. 1993, pp. 6–7.

Shaughnessy, M. P. *Errors and Expectations: A Guide for the Teacher of Basic Writing.* New York: Oxford University Press, 1977.

CAROLE E. BARROWMAN *is associate professor of English, chair of the Communication Ability Department, and a member of the Assessment Council, Alverno College.*

# INDEX

# ORDERING INFORMATION

NEW DIRECTIONS FOR HIGHER EDUCATION is a series of paperback books that provides timely information and authoritative advice about major issues and administrative problems confronting every institution. Books in the series are published quarterly in Spring, Summer, Fall, and Winter and are available for purchase by subscription and individually.

SUBSCRIPTIONS cost $52.00 for individuals (a savings of 35 percent over single-copy prices) and $79.00 for institutions, agencies, and libraries. Standing orders are accepted. New York residents, add local tax for subscriptions. (For subscriptions outside the United States, add $7.00 for shipping via surface mail or $25.00 for air mail. Orders *must be prepaid* in U.S. dollars by check drawn on a U.S. bank or charged to VISA, MasterCard, or American Express.)

SINGLE COPIES cost $20.00 plus shipping (see below) when payment accompanies order. California, New Jersey, New York, and Washington, D.C., residents, please include appropriate sales tax. Canadian residents, add GST and any local taxes. Billed orders will be charged shipping and handling. No billed shipments to post office boxes. (Orders from outside the United States *must be prepaid* in U.S. dollars by check drawn on a U.S. bank or charged to VISA, MasterCard, or American Express.)

SHIPPING (SINGLE COPIES ONLY): $20.00 and under, add $3.50; to $50.00, add $4.50; to $75.00, add $5.50; to $100.00, add $6.50; to $150.00, add $7.50; over $150.00, add $8.50.

ALL PRICES are subject to change.

DISCOUNTS FOR QUANTITY ORDERS are available. Please write to the address below for information.

ALL ORDERS must include either the name of an individual or an official purchase order number. Please submit your order as follows:
    *Subscriptions:* specify series and year subscription is to begin
    *Single copies:* include individual title code (such as HE82)

MAIL ALL ORDERS TO:
    Jossey-Bass Publishers
    350 Sansome Street
    San Francisco, California 94104-1342

FOR SUBSCRIPTION SALES OUTSIDE OF THE UNITED STATES, contact any international subscription agency or Jossey-Bass directly.

OTHER TITLES AVAILABLE IN THE
NEW DIRECTIONS FOR HIGHER EDUCATION SERIES
*Martin Kramer*, Editor-in-Chief